"Now keep your seats, gals! We are going to talk about a very delicate subject—how to catch a man! Whatever you do, don't let the men find out what is going on here. This is just between us girls …"

You are listening to Carolyn Hobbs talking to a group of Christian young ladies, all of whom are seeking the Lord's will for their lives and most of whom are hoping that includes a husband—and soon!

Sprinkled liberally throughout the audience are married women of various ages who have come to hear this successful wife tell how the Word of God can help them fulfill the role the Lord has chosen for them.

Now for the first time the essence of these talks is offered in book form. This book can make you a better wife, a better woman, a better Christian. Enjoy it.

—The Publishers

"And he loved her"

Carolyn Hobbs

Bob Jones University Press, Inc.
Greenville, South Carolina 29614

And He Loved Her
by Carolyn Hobbs

© 1979 Bob Jones University Press, Inc.
ISBN: 0-89084-113-6
Printed in the United States of America.

Acknowledgment

To Dayton, my husband of twenty-seven years, for giving me the privilege of being his helpmeet in the Lord's service and for making our home a touch of heaven on earth.

To Elmer Rumminger, Shelba Buchanan, and others of the publisher's staff for their assistance and expertise.

To Child Evangelism Fellowship, Inc., for permission to use the poem "Lasting Treasures," by Billy Davis, from *Child Evangelism* magazine.

To Faith, Prayer, and Tract League for the poem "In the Morning," by Ralph Cushman.

To dear family and friends who have been a blessing to my life and contributed in many ways to the development of this book.

About the author

In addition to her duties as a homemaker and mother of two children who are now married, Carolyn McVay Hobbs has served as a school teacher, curriculum writer, and vice-principal, and is currently the coordinator of schools for Santa Rosa Christian School and Century Christian School. She is a frequent and popular speaker for women's meetings, youth groups, conferences, and Christian school convention seminars. Children know and love her as "Aunt Carolyn," the director and storyteller of "The Children's Bible Club," a fifteen-minute weekly radio broadcast heard on nearly thirty stations. She has written nine books used in children's work. An accomplished pianist and capable secretary, she has contributed greatly to her husband's ministry over the years.

Mrs. Hobbs's primary responsibility, however, is that of wife and helpmeet to her husband, Dr. Dayton Hobbs. Dr. Hobbs is pastor of Grace Fellowship Church in Milton, Florida, and president of Santa Rosa and Century Christian Schools. He edits the monthly fundamentalist paper, *The Projector,* and has written several articles and books on Christian education. He received an honorary doctor's degree from Bob Jones University in 1968, and has been recognized in *Personalities of the South.*

Dr. and Mrs. Hobbs are graduates of Bob Jones University and recipients of the University's Alumni Award in recognition of their accomplishments and Christian service. They are vibrant examples of the challenge set forth in this book: a man who is dedicated to the will of God and a wife who enthusiastically supports him in his ministry.

Contents

Introduction xiii

1 Genesis 24: Rebekah 1

2 I Samuel 25: Abigail 49

3 II Kings 4: The Shunammite 89

4 Proverbs 31: The Virtuous Woman 123

Conclusion 171

"And Isaac brought her into his mother Sarah's tent, and took Rebekah, and she became his wife; and he loved her."

—Genesis 24:67

Introduction

Of course, you want a husband. The desire comes installed as standard equipment on all female models of the species. You try to look innocent and you don't talk about it much, but the truth remains that you want a husband. Your mother had one; your grandmother had one; and your great-grandmother had one. It really has become a family tradition, and who are you to break family tradition?

Love and marriage are the heart's desires of every girl. Now it is not always the Lord's will for every girl to be married. God has some precious gems that He singles out for a special calling, but in this book I am talking especially to those whom God would bring together and unite with a man in holy matrimony. So keep your seats, girls! We are entering that delicious, mysterious, plot-laying, trap-setting subject of how to catch a man!

Chapter 1

Genesis 24: Rebekah

The perfect strategy for catching a man is laid out in the twenty-fourth chapter of Genesis. This precious chapter is one of those classics you treasure more each time you read it. The whole chapter is a beautiful picture of God's plan of salvation and His provision for us. Abraham represents God the Father, who shows His perfect love for His beloved Son and His perfect plan in bringing the bride for His Son. We see God's plan of salvation in Abraham. Isaac represents the Son, Jesus Christ, the only begotten of the Father. He portrays the beloved Son of Whom God said, "This is my beloved Son, hear him." Isaac, the son in whom all the father's riches are vested, speaks of Christ in Whom "should all fulness dwell" (Col. 1:19). In Him are all "the riches of his grace" (Eph. 1:7). Isaac is a type of Him in Whom "dwelleth all the fulness of the Godhead bodily" (Col. 2:9). The bride is a picture of the church, all believers who come to Jesus Christ by faith and become partakers of "the exceeding riches of his grace" (Eph. 2:7).

Perhaps the hero of the story is the person introduced in Genesis 24:2, the eldest servant. Verse 1 says, "And Abraham was old, and well stricken in age: and the Lord had blessed Abraham in all things." Verse 2: "And Abraham said unto his eldest servant of his house, that ruled over all that he had." We see in this eldest servant a picture of God's Holy Spirit, the One Who represents or testifies of the Son. When this eldest servant took the long trip to find a wife for Isaac, never did he refer to himself, never did he exalt himself; he always represented the son, whose master had sent him to seek a bride. What a beautiful picture this is of the Holy Spirit. Jesus said, "But when the Comforter is come . . . , he shall testify of me" (John 15:26). When the Holy Spirit is present, He is never saying, "Look at the Holy Spirit." He is always saying, "Look at the Lord Jesus Christ." "When he, the Spirit of truth, is come . . . he shall not speak of himself; . . . he shall glorify me"(John 16:13-14). The Holy Spirit works to bring the bride for the Son, never exalting Himself but always the Son. So, the Holy Spirit's work of bringing you to repentance, testifying of the Lord Jesus Christ, and bringing you to faith in Him is all-important, and there is really no use to continue in the chapter until you have met Jesus Christ at the cross, having been drawn to Him through the power of the Holy Spirit.

> *My faith has found a resting place,*
> *Not in device nor creed;*
> *I trust the Ever-living One,*
> *His wounds for me shall plead.*

I need no other argument,
I need no other plea,
It is enough that Jesus died,
And that He died for me.

—Lidie H. Edmunds

So we have seen the main characters: Abraham, who represents God the Father; Isaac, who represents God the Son; and the eldest servant, who represents the Holy Spirit. But for the purpose of our study, we want to consider the young woman whom the servant found to be the bride for Isaac.

Salvation is by grace. Everything we have is by grace. If God brings you a husband, that, too, will be by His grace. As every eye-pleasing, mouth-watering, gourmet dish that you will prepare to please your future husband has a perfect set of ingredients with an exact order of mixing them together, so in God's bringing two people together in marriage, there are certain ingredients that must be put together in the right amount and in the right order. That order is what we want to notice in this chapter. You see, if two people come together in a haphazard courtship and have a haphazard wedding, the marriage that follows may be worse than haphazard; it may be a disaster! We have to follow the Word of God. We have to go by what God would have us do. Let's see how God worked it out in this young girl's life.

In verses 3 and 4 of Genesis 24, Abraham spoke to the servant and said, "And I will make thee swear by the Lord, the God of heaven, and the God of the earth, that thou shalt not take a wife unto my son of the daughters of the Canaanites, among whom I dwell: But thou shalt go unto my country, and to my kindred, and take a wife unto my son Isaac." The desire of the father was that the son have a bride of his own faith. This is all-important if you are a Christian girl. The first requirement is that you have a husband who is a Christian. "Be not unequally yoked together with unbelievers" is a principle of the Word of God that you have heard time and time again. Do not be tempted to date or spend time with young men who are not Christians. It can only detract from your work and testimony. You are tempted to think, "Well, I won't fall for that guy, but he is fun to be with, and he is nice. I'll just spend a little time." Look out! Settle it once and for all that you will not date or marry someone who is not a Christian.

The father said, "First of all we want someone of like precious faith. Don't get anybody in this land where we live. Don't get one of the heathen Canaanites, whose beliefs are contrary to God's Word, who is not a Christian and not dedicated wholly to the God of Heaven." The servant answered, "Well, what if she won't come with me?" That was a reasonable question because all young ladies are not willing to do right; all young ladies are not determined to do God's will at all costs. Abraham said, "If she won't come, then that's not your fault; you will not be bound to my oath." How dangerous it is when the Holy Spirit comes to woo a person, convicts of sin, and seeks to win him to the Lord Jesus Christ and the person says, "I will not." What a fearful thing! It is possible to reject and resist the Holy Spirit's speaking in our hearts, but then we must take the blame. It is not God's fault, it is not the fault of the Holy Spirit, and it is not the fault of the Lord Jesus Christ. It's our own fault if we resist His love and the wooing of the Holy Spirit in our hearts. We must take the consequences.

Orders were plain; preparations were made; and at last the tremendous operation was underway.

> Verses 10-14: "And the servant took ten camels of the camels of his master, and departed; for all the goods of his master were in his hand: and he arose, and went to Mesopotamia, unto the city of Nahor. And he made his camels to kneel down without the city by a well of water at the time of the evening, even the time that women go out to draw water. And he said, O Lord God of my master Abraham, I pray thee, send me good speed this day, and shew kindness unto my master Abraham. Behold, I stand here by the well of water; and the daughters of the men of the city come out to draw water: And let it come to pass, that the damsel to whom I shall say, Let down thy pitcher, I pray thee, that I may drink; and she shall say, Drink, and I will give thy camels drink also; let the same be she that thou hast appointed for thy servant Isaac; and thereby shall I know that thou hast shewed kindness unto my master."

Notice verse 15: "And it came to pass, before he had done speaking," he barely had the words out of his mouth, before, "Behold, Rebekah came out."

Promptness

The first winning quality about Rebekah was that
she was on time. I would say the first rule of catching
a man is to be faithful to your present duties and
responsibilities. The deed that Rebekah did that day
was probably a routine responsibility that she had
carried out ever since she was big enough to carry
one of those big clay pots on her shoulder. From the
time she was a little thing, her mother had no doubt
taught her how to walk to keep that jar balanced.
Some women in Oriental countries balance the jars
on top of their heads. It is amazing. A modern
Christian mother may try to teach her daughter
how to walk gracefully by putting a book on her
head and teaching her how to place her feet, but
how the Oriental girls ever walk under the weight
and awkwardness of their huge clay jars is a
mystery. Rebekah carried her jar on her shoulder.
She had to balance it on one side with her head and
on the other side with her arm. She had walked all
the way from home with her empty pitcher and had
come to the well, "even the time that women go out
to draw water." Rebekah was prompt. She knew
when it was time to be at the well, and she was there
apparently first. It was an everyday responsibility.
There was no glamor to it. She didn't know that
there was going to be someone special at the well
that day. She was just faithful to her responsibility.
Dr. Bob Jones, Sr. used to tell students to be faithful
today: do what you are supposed to do today, and
ten years from now, you will be where God wants
you. Don't get ruffled and worried about God's will
for your life. Settle down. Do today what

you know is God's will. Get the dishes done today. Do the work that is before you today. Roll out when the alarm clock goes off today. Keep your schedule today. Meet your responsibilities today. Be prompt and faithful. Go to the well on time today, and God will open the right door and bring the right person to you at the right time.

Rebekah knew how to be prompt. At the time when the girls were supposed to be at the well to draw water, Rebekah was the first one there. Say, if you are late on every other date, you will keep on being late. You may even (heaven forbid) be late to the altar! But if you're late now, if it doesn't mean anything to meet your date on time before you're married, what makes you think you will have supper prepared on time after you are married? You will be two days behind with the ironing after you're married. You will be two weeks behind with the housework. Why would a young man want to marry a girl who stands him up and says, "Just a minute, I'll be right there"? Then thirty minutes later, she comes tripping down the stairs. He may look at her fluttering eyelashes and be taken in by her rolling eyeballs, but it won't last long.

Do you remember the children's nursery rhyme:

> A diller, a dollar,
> A ten o'clock scholar,
> What makes you come so soon?
> You used to come at ten o'clock,
> And now you come at noon.

The little scholar had a bad flaw in his character. He started out being pokey and late and then had a relapse. So it is with any fault or sin in our lives. Sin that is not judged and forsaken does not stay dormant but becomes worse, getting a tighter grip on our lives and doing more and more damage. Faults which may not seem serious in the beginning become heavy weights which hurt our testimony and hinder our service if not judged and committed to the Lord.

Rebekah was on time, and that is a trait that a Christian young woman should develop. If you are late while you are young, you will get worse when you get older. It will be harder to be at Sunday school on time after you are married and also have dinner to cook in the morning so it will be done when you come home from church. It will be harder yet when you have children and you have to get them and yourself ready for Sunday school and cook dinner too. And it will be harder still when you have to get yourself ready and the children ready and cook dinner for your family and company too. Being prompt doesn't get easier. Train yourself while you are young, before you marry, to be prompt, to meet your responsibilities, and not to take any schedule lightly.

Respect

You must know this about Rebekah too: she honored her parents. Apparently there was no argument about her going to the well. She may have been the only water boy in the family, I don't know, but there is no indication that she griped about it. She carried out the responsibilities that her father required of her, and thus she honored her parents. She obeyed her father's command, and, you will notice, when the servant began to ask, "Whose daughter art thou?" she was glad to tell who her father was and what the family ancestry was.

Rebekah did not know this strange servant. If resentment or bitterness had been in her heart, she could have slandered her father by saying, "Yeah, my Daddy, you ought to see him. He makes me come down here at six o'clock every night and carry this big old water jug. I'm really overworked. Nobody at home understands me." No! She told in an honorable way of her father and showed respect for her family. Now, any young man who is wise will not spend time with or allow himself to fall in love with a girl who shows no respect for her family. I do not know what your family background is, but you see to it that you honor your father and mother. A girl who will dishonor her parents or who will berate or degrade her parents to her boyfriend because she thinks it will make him sorry for her or will build his ego will later on degrade her husband when he crosses her. She'll go home to Mama and start bad-mouthing her husband. Any girl who does not honor and respect her parents will not honor and respect her husband. Rebekah knew how to obey and give proper honor to her parents, showing true loyalty.

Beauty

Not only was Rebekah prompt, but she "was very fair to look upon" (Gen. 24:16). This gal was a real beauty. Her beauty was not fake. It was not painted on the outside and done up like a Christmas package just to fool a man or make him think she was a beautiful doll. There has been more than one home ruined by a young man's marrying a girl who was the town beauty—he thought. I remember a certain wedding at which some of the men who attended saw the bride and gave wolf whistles. They thought she was a living doll. But after the wedding,

I imagine, there was more than one time that young husband wished he could turn her loose and let one of those other fellows have her. Her beauty did not make her able to stand up under the trials of sickness, hard times, and difficulties at home or at work. To make a good marriage takes more than skin-deep beauty. The prayer of Christian young women should be: "Let the beauty of the Lord our God be upon us" (Ps. 90:17). This is true, lasting beauty which becomes more lovely with the passing years. The money spent on makeup and so-called beauty aids every year must come to an astronomical figure. Now don't misunderstand me; I'm not against a little makeup. Some of us need a little to cover up the "uglies," but when your face and eyes begin to advertise "Makeup, makeup," and you look like a neon sign flashing, that is beyond the framework of being gracious. Makeup ought not to be our sign. It's not outward beauty that counts; it is character of the heart.

Proper Clothing

Rebekah was modestly and appropriately dressed, even though she didn't know she was going to have the opportunity to meet someone who was going to line her up with a husband that day. She was dressed for work, but she didn't come out to the well wearing something that made her look like a man. The unisex thrust is one of the plagues of our times. God expects men to look like men and women to look like ladies. In a recent crossword puzzle in an airline magazine, the definition given for "slacks" was "unisex apparel." The world knows what it is about, but some Christians don't want to admit it. There may be some activities, such as going to a skating party or playing in a ball game or painting a high ceiling, when slacks or culottes would be appropriate and even more modest, but ordinarily a woman's responsibility is to wear dresses and look modest, and to fill her role as a responsible mother or wife in the home. There is just no excuse for a Christian woman to go around "showing herself." Have you been to the grocery store and noticed the sights lately? I know you have. I don't know what women would have done without double knits! The women get broader and broader and if the knits didn't stretch with them, oooh, the world couldn't contain the sight! Really, it is pitiful! But if you find yourself gawking, what do men do? I was in the post office recently when in came a big, sweet thing in shorts. The act that followed was classic. I'm sure the men wouldn't have appreciated my watching them, but I was observing their reaction instead of the girl. They weren't young men either, they were old cronies, and every head turned and every eye followed the big swingin' gal. Now if that's the kind of attention you want, just help yourself. We will know to just what kind of category you belong. But a Christian girl ought to be modestly dressed in every situation. There is no time when a Christian girl can set aside virtue and modesty and say, "Oh well, forget it. I'm just going to be me." Well, you might just as well be "you" the rest of the time, too, because that's what you really are.

It was probably hot at the well, and Rebekah's work was hard. She probably could have slung off some of her clothing with the excuse, "Well, it's just too hot!" But no, she came out modestly dressed.

This is very important for us women. It's also important to remember if the Lord should give you little girls to rear for Him, you should train them early to dress modestly. Don't wait until they get to high school and then hope that they will learn modesty. It ought to be second nature by then. Bring them up with the right principles of modest dress. Rebekah was dressed for work when she came to the well to draw water.

Purity

But verse 16 tells us something else about Rebekah: Rebekah was pure. She was "a virgin, neither had any man known her." What a blessing it is to find a young lady with clean standards who has not thrown away her affections. Hold your standards in line with the Word of God. Live with the idea that you are saving yourself for the husband that God has for you sometime in the future. When that somebody comes along, you don't want him to think, "Well, I wonder who else has held her. I wonder who else has petted or loved her. I wonder to whom she has thrown her kisses before me." No! When you marry, you are not going to want bad memories or to want to think, "Oh, my husband is so wonderful," and then in the back of your mind think, "But remember when..." No, God wants virgins, women who hold their affections for the husband whom the Lord gives in His time. A song that was popular during World War II was about a girl whose boyfriend had been shipped overseas in military service. He was far away, and she was lonely, but she rejected all attention and invitations from other interested men with the simple phrase, "I'm saving myself for Bill." Now that was not a

Christian song, but the principle was right. She had standards. She knew what it meant to be loyal and true.

Energy

Rebekah was an energetic girl. She went down to the well as she had done every day, filled her pitcher, and came up again. Now, you have to remember that those big jars could have easily weighed many pounds. Have you ever carried a five-gallon can of gasoline? When I was a child, I used to tend the chickens and carry a bucket of grain or water in each hand. You square your shoulders and walk tall, so you won't get hunched over. By the time you walk from the barn to the chicken house you're tired, right? Okay, imagine taking that same weight and heaving it up above your shoulder and carrying it. Now perhaps you can feel Rebekah's load. In those days, some wells had circular stone banisters around the top, and the bucket was let down by a rope to the water. Apparently this well, however, had a passage dug away with steps built from ground level down to water level so that the people walked down steps all the way to the water below. Verse 16 says, "She went down to the well, and filled her pitcher, and came up." Now how long those steps were I don't know, but there are still some wells like that in the Holy Land. The pool of Bethesda was such a well. The steps could have been long and difficult. However long and difficult they were, Rebekah went all the way down, filled her pitcher, heaved it up on her shoulder, and walked all the way up the steps again. Now watch what happens. The servant ran to meet her and said, "Let me, I pray thee, drink a little water of thy pitcher."

And she graciously said, "Drink, my lord." You
know, she could have said, "What nerve! Who do
you think I am! Who was your servant last year at
this time? Go get your own water! You're a man;
you're as healthy as I am! I'll be switched if I'm going
to haul water for you! It's bad enough to haul it for
my pa!" But she let the pitcher down and gave him
water.

Now notice what else she did. She said, "Drink,"
and she *hasted!* This girl ran. You see, she put
everything into whatever she was doing. If she had
to get water, she ran up and down the steps. She
ran, she hasted, and in verse 20 again it says she
"ran." She let down her pitcher on her hand, poured
the water out and gave him a drink, and then she
said, "I will draw water for thy camels also, until they
have done drinking." Now that is amazing. That's
"hospitality plus," I'd say. Have you ever watched a
camel? They say that a camel after a good hard
day's travel can drink a bathtub-size amount of
water. How many gallons does a bathtub hold? How
many gallons were in this pitcher? It could hardly
have been more than five because she couldn't have
carried much more on her shoulder. Say the pitcher
would hold five gallons; then a bathtub full would
hold fifty gallons easily. To water just one camel,
how many trips up and down would Rebekah have
made? But she watered ten camels and hasted the
whole time. No wonder the man stood back and
watched in amazement. I would have, too. Do you
see what a willing heart she had, and what a willing
worker Rebekah was? Her attitude was not, "Look
out, I've got to hurry home, and anyhow this
pitcher's heavy. Go get a bucket and water your

own dumb, old camels. I hate the ugly things anyhow!" But Rebekah "hasted" to bring water to them. She was energetic.

Unselfishness

From Beersheba to Nahor in Mesopotamia was from 450 to 500 miles. If the camels had made twenty-five to thirty miles a day, they had traveled fifteen to twenty days. Guess who was tired! Guess who needed lots of water! Look what a job Rebekah voluntarily took on herself when she said, "And I'll water your camels, too." I don't know how many trips up and down those steps she made with that huge jar to fill up those thirsty camels. I imagine her shoulder was black and blue by the time she finished. But Rebekah was not concerned about herself; she was considering what she could do for somebody else. She was showing herself to be unselfish, hospitable, friendly, and gracious. She was doing all she could do for someone else. What man wouldn't want a young lady like that? What man wouldn't be delighted over a girl whose concern was for others and who was always seeking to be a voluntary worker? That's the kind of girl who is needed in God's work. A young man who is going to be in God's service needs a wife who will not spare herself but will go with him, stand with him, support him, and always be giving one hundred and ten percent.

Rebekah not only was a volunteer worker, but she took on jobs that were bigger than she was. She was working when nobody else was working. There are some people who will get in and really go if there are fifteen other people helping with the job, but they are quick to let you know, "I'm not going to do it by myself." Rebekah was willing to do the job alone if need be. As far as I know, the man didn't help a bit. She was up and down those steps countless times, working when nobody else was working. That's the kind of women for whom the Lord is looking. He is looking for those who will be in His service willingly, ones who don't have to be begged, ones who serve unselfishly. God is looking for women who are looking ahead, seeing the jobs that need to be done whether at home or in the Lord's work, the church or the school. There are a "jillion" jobs that need doing, but there are some people who never see them. Then there are others who see them ahead of time and get busy. You never hear from that kind, but they are getting the job done. That's the kind of people the Lord wants us to be. There are some times in the Lord's work when you just have to move faster than you ever knew you could move. "The king's business required haste" (I Sam. 21:8).

Hospitality

Abraham's servant had asked her whose daughter she was, and she had said, "I'm the daughter of Bethuel the son of Milcah." Now notice verse 25, "She said moreover unto him, We have both straw and provender enough, and room to lodge in." Would you believe this girl? She has not only bent over backwards to help the servant; now she is inviting him home. This means sharing supper or else cooking more potatoes. This means making up an extra bed, being sure the bedroom is clean and the bathroom is in order. She is taking on more work in order to be hospitable. You have to tip your hat to her mother, though. She reared Rebekah to be like this. The Bible says of a bishop, who is a leader in the Lord's work, that he should be "given to hospitality" (I Tim. 3:2) and be "a lover of hospitality" (Titus 1:8). I Peter 4:9 tells us to "use hospitality one to another without grudging." Hebrews 13:2 says, "Be not forgetful to entertain strangers: for thereby some have entertained angels unawares." Some Christians are too clannish. They seem to feel, "This is for me and my family, us four and no more, and nobody else had better come through our door." But what a difference there was in Rebekah's household. She didn't have to worry whether it would be all right with Daddy to bring an extra guest for supper who needed a place to spend the night. Her family had been doing that over the years. They had a home where God's people could come and be welcome. She knew this man was a Christian by his testimony: how he prayed and how God had led him all the way. She knew that this man would be welcome in her father's home. Bethuel and his wife had reared the children to be hospitable. We know this because Laban, Rebekah's brother, came out and met Rebekah and the servant and said, "Come in; there's plenty. Let me help you." Bethuel's household cared for the whole caravan: the camels, the servants, and the servant of Abraham. God's people ought to be hospitable. People ought to know when they come to your town that they have a place to stay at your house if they need it. Don't raise your children to be selfish and feel, "This is my room, these are my toys, this is my supper, and I won't share with anybody."

I remember preacher Culver, an old-time Kansas preacher, whose home always had the welcome mat

out for friends or strangers. Often unexpected
guests arrived. Times were hard, but one Sunday
the mother fixed a chicken for dinner. The family
itself was big, and, you guessed it, that day
unexpected company came, too. They all gathered
around the table, and the father asked the blessing.
After prayer the youngest boy surveyed the
situation and murmured, "Too many people for one
little chickie!" Perhaps he thought he would get
shortchanged, but I'm sure he didn't suffer. The
Lord has a way of making a little go a long way in a
home where Jesus Christ is put first and where
there is true Christian, unselfish love.

Bethuel's home was a place where God's people
found a warm welcome. Make your home that way if
you are a Christian mother or wife. Make your
home a haven where your husband feels at ease at
suppertime if he wants to bring home his friend or
relative or business associate or some child that he
found on the street and won to the Lord. Be sure he
can bring him home for supper and know that he will
find a welcome there, that you won't storm for five
minutes and be two-faced in the kitchen saying, "I
don't know why you brought that person!" and then
to the person say, "Oh, how do you do. We're so
glad to have you." Woe to that household. Make
your home like Bethuel's, a place where God's
people are welcome.

Gratitude

We can learn from Abraham's servant too. As
we go through the chapter, notice his constant
gratitude. Every little bit, he was bowing down and
praising the Lord for answering prayer. Blessed is
the person who has a thankful heart. If anybody

does anything for you, be thankful. I have seen some children to whom I believe you could give a five-dollar bill, and it wouldn't cross their minds to say "thank you." They just don't know what "thank you" means. Why is it so hard to teach kids to say "thank you"? At all times, by all means, teach your children to be thankful, not just for the big things, but for every little thing, for "every good gift and every perfect gift is from above, and cometh down from the Father of lights" (James 1:17). The best way to teach children to be thankful is for them to hear their parents say "thank you" for everything anyone does for them.

As Rebekah came flying home, Laban came out to meet her and saw the earring and the two golden bracelets the servant had given her. After all she had done for him, the servant rewarded her with something she could treasure, but Rebekah hadn't expected a reward. She hadn't expected pay. When she started that big job, she didn't bargain for how much she was going to get paid! "Well, I'll do it for a dollar per camel." She met the man's need out of the graciousness of her heart because she wanted to help him. Afterwards she got another reward that she hadn't expected. It's that way in God's business. You don't make bargains with God Almighty, but when you are faithful and diligent in His work, He more than rewards His children.

Dependability
Abraham's servant, like Rebekah, was dependable in fulfilling his responsibilities. After the camels were ungirded and tended, the weary travelers washed and had a sumptuous supper set before them. Blessings on Abraham's servant again!

Then the servant said in verse 33: "I will not eat, until I have told mine errand." He was a faithful, dependable servant. He put the work of his master ahead of his own hungry stomach; he wouldn't even eat until he had carried out his master's command. Oh, if we could learn to put the Lord's will and the Lord's work ahead of our own weak flesh. It's so easy to look out for ourselves. We put off the Lord's work while looking out for our own personal pleasure or security. We plan on what we want to spend our money for instead of asking God how it could be used in His work. The servant put his master's will ahead of his own needs, ahead of his own comforts, ahead of everything.

In the next few verses, the servant tells how the Lord blessed Abraham with silver and gold, herds and servants. Then he told about the son and how that all the master had belonged to the son. He testified to God's leadership in his task. Notice verse 40: "The Lord, before whom I walk, will send his angel with thee." Say, did you know you have angels with you if you're God's child? If you're yielded to Him, God sends His angel before to make a way for you. Now some folks don't thank the Lord for the angel or pay any attention to the path the angel or the Lord or His Spirit makes. They're too busy running interference for themselves, making their own path. They say, "I want to do this. I want to be that. I want certain things for my house. I want my time for myself," instead of saying, "Lord, here I am. I'm not much, but take me and use me. If I burn out for the Lord, that will be all right." It's surely better than rusting out, isn't it? And rusting out is what happens when we protect ourselves and say that we don't have but a certain amount of time or energy we can give to the Lord.

The servant finishes telling the story by relating the proceedings at the well: how the virgin came, how he met her, and how she offered not only him drink but also the camels, just exactly as he had prayed. "And before I had done speaking in mine heart, behold, Rebekah came forth with her pitcher on her shoulder; and she went down unto the well, and drew water, and I said unto her, Let me drink, I pray thee. And she made haste . . . and said, Drink, and I will give thy camels drink also." He told how he inquired about whose daughter she was and put the earring and the bracelets in her hands, and said, "I bowed down my head, and worshipped the Lord, and blessed the Lord God of my master Abraham, which had led me in the right way."

Now comes the bomb! All this has been leading up to one thing, and don't you think Rebekah has been standing over in the corner wondering about the outcome of this whole episode? When she was watering camels, she didn't suspect any of this. By this time though, I imagine her heart was racing. I imagine she caught her breath when the servant said, "If ye will deal kindly and truly with my master, tell me: and if not, tell me; that I may turn to the right hand, or to the left." In other words he was saying, "If you'll let Rebekah go home and be Isaac's wife, say yea. If not, say nay, and I'll act accordingly." It was a simple proposition.

Now nobody asked Rebekah's opinion about it. I imagine she was doing some praying! But isn't it wonderful that she had faithful parents who were concerned about the outcome? Bethuel gave the answer without hesitation. He had been considering the matter all the way through the servant's testimony. He had been listening for indications of the Lord's will for Rebekah's life. He had been praying too. In one way this situation was no surprise. He hadn't waited for this decision to arise to start praying. I'm sure Bethuel had been praying about God's will for Rebekah's life and possible marriage for years, preparing his daughter for the time when God would give her a husband. Both Laban and Bethuel answered, "The thing proceedeth from the Lord: we cannot speak unto thee bad or good."

I know a little sharp stab went across Bethuel's heart. There was beautiful Rebekah, the daughter he had loved all these years. To think that all of a sudden she would be gone was no easy thing. Abraham lived 450-500 miles from home. Bethuel might never see his daughter again. Yet he thought that if this was God's will for her life, he could not interfere. He could not say "good" because he knew he would miss his daughter's sweet smile, her gentle laughter, and her willing help at home; but he could not say "bad" because more than anything else, he wanted her to do the Lord's will. Can you understand his love and heart? Blessed is the young woman who has a Christian father who desires to rear his daughter for the Lord.

Once again, the servant showed a thankful heart by bowing himself to the earth and worshiping the Lord. Then he brought forth silver, jewels of gold, and raiment and gave them to Rebekah and her family. They ate and drank, and he and his men tarried all night.

What a celebration that must have been! I doubt that Rebekah could eat, though. Her head must have been swimming! Up to that very day she had been faithful to her responsibilities, and now all of a sudden, she was engaged—all but hitched! The whole matter was settled, and in just a little while she would be going away to be married. What a night it must have been!

It was the wee hours of the morning before anybody went to bed, but when they rose in the morning, Abraham's servant said, "Send me away unto my master." Rebekah's mother said, "Let the damsel abide with us a few days, at the least ten; after that she shall go." Oh, you can understand that. She had a mother's heart. This whole thing was such a shock. She had reared the child, rocked her in the cradle, watched her toddle and finally walk and run. Little Rebekah was always under her feet in the kitchen, and her mother taught her how to cook. They had had those close, precious talks that mothers and daughters have. They had talked about many things while washing dishes, and the mother taught her how to fry meat to keep it from tasting like leather and how to stir a cake to keep it light. I imagine they were close; a mother and daughter get that way. So it was a mother's heart that wanted to hold on to Rebekah just a few more days, but it was a dedicated heart that was willing to let her go. Blessed is the mother who bears her children, rocks them, disciplines, loves, rears them one hundred percent for only one purpose—to have them entirely dedicated to the service and will of God. That, my dears, is success.

Proper Motivation

At last the time came for Rebekah to make a decision. "And he said unto them, Hinder me not, seeing the Lord hath prospered my way; send me away that I may go to my master." He said, "I don't have time to tarry. I did my job; now I have to get back home." Rebekah's family must have had aching hearts, but they said, "We will call the damsel, and enquire at her mouth." Now we're going to see how yielded Miss Rebekah is: whether she is willing to go all the way with the Lord or if she is going to hang on to Mama's apron strings. You'll see that Rebekah made the decision, and then she stuck with it. She didn't wring her hands or cry or squall; she simply said, "I'll go."

Rebekah had to have the right motive, or this arrangement would never have been agreeable. Every girl ought to check her motives for wanting to marry. It's so easy to have a wrong motive. Anything less than true love for the Lord and for the man that God brings to you is not a justifiable motive for marriage. If a girl has a motive any lower than that, the marriage will crumble when the going gets tough.

One invalid motive for marriage is money. Oh, you say, "That's ridiculous; I wouldn't even consider that." But there are some girls, even Christian girls, who think, "I just want to find a wealthy husband so I can live on easy street. I've seen so many Christian women who have had to work hard all their lives. I don't want my life to be like that. I hope to find a man in the insurance business or a banker or a doctor who can provide everything so I won't have to work my head off all my life." Now girls will never say that out loud, but that thought filters through some girls' minds. They do not want to sacrifice for the Lord or anyone else. Check your motives.

Some young women seek marriage to get out from under parental authority. They are tired of living at home and having Mama tell them what to do and having Dad expect them home at a given hour. They want to be out from under authority. "If I were married," they think, "I'd be under my own roof. I'd be my own boss." But that motive will not make a young woman shoulder responsibility and face reality in living. Check your motive.

Some young ladies get what I call "senior panic." They might not necessarily be in college when the crisis hits, but it is about college age when they think, "If I don't get married now, I'm sunk. If I don't catch a man now, I'll probably never catch one." So they marry the first thing that passes by in britches, just so they can say they conquered. They are afraid of what somebody might think if they don't catch a man. Let me tell you something. There are worse things in the world than being single. There is nothing more wonderful this side of heaven than being married to the right man in God's will, but there's nothing worse this side of hell than being married to the wrong man and getting yourself tied up for life in a union that is out of the will of God. I don't care how much money your man has, how handsome he is, what a catch he seems to be. If the marriage is not God's will, it won't work. You won't be happy, and you will end up ruining a man's life.

The only right motive for marriage is true love brought by God to a man and woman who are totally dedicated to the Lord. You had better be

certain you want God's will no matter what the cost.
You had better come to the point where you are
honestly willing to say, "Lord, maybe I'm not
supposed to be married. If that's the way You want
it, that's okay with me. If You want me to be
married, then You bring the right one. I leave the
matter in Your hands." That prayer has to be made
in your heart with real meaning, not just with words.
Then, if God brings that right one along, you can
marry knowing that marriage is God's will for you,
knowing you love that man more than your own self.
Now, if at any point you are still looking out for
yourself, don't get married. If in your heart there are
still any thoughts for self, if you don't love that man
more than you love life itself, if his work and his
calling don't mean more than your own life's blood
and flesh, if looking out for his welfare doesn't mean
more than yours, then leave him alone. Don't mess
up his ministry and life's work. Stay out of his path
unless you love him beyond anything in this world,
including yourself. Jesus Christ has to be first in
both your lives, and next to the Lord your husband
has to be Number One. You must love him so much
that you would rather be with him than anybody
else; you would rather give him more attention than
anybody else. He has to be, as far as this earth is
concerned, everything to you. Then you can work
together in the Lord's will.

Before my husband and I were married, we loved
each other and we knew it. Being a little older than
some when we met, we seemed to know quite soon
that our love was real, and before too long, the
wedding date was set. We loved each other
sincerely and deeply, yet I remember praying more

than once, "Lord, You know my heart. You know I love him; but if in any way I would hinder his work or his ministry, do something to stop the plans now. He loves you, Lord, with all his heart; he is dedicated to your will, and if I would get in the way of that, do something to cancel it out." (And my heart was pounding; I was scared that the Lord would stop it, terrified to think, "What if He does cancel it?") But I had to be honest with the Lord, see? And that's what your attitude must be toward the man that God has for you. Remember the order of marriage is not "him for you," but "you for him." You are to be his helpmeet to help him in his work.

The story gets better and richer as you go along, but only because Rebekah made the right choice. There were unknown and uncharted waters ahead, just as there are in any marriage. Before the marriage and the pretty wedding and all the frills, things look rosy, but suppose the next year you don't have any money. Suppose the next year the baby gets so sick you don't know what the outcome is going to be. Can you stand together no matter what comes? You have to love him enough to stand with him no matter how thick the troubles. It has to be you and he, by the grace of God. Now if you don't love him that much, if you don't respect him that much, if you haven't found one you can pray for and dedicate your time to that much, then leave him alone. Tell him, "Thanks a lot. I think the world of you, but I can't join you for life," and go on your way. Don't mess up a man's life and ministry. Don't join him at the altar unless you're willing to dedicate all to Christ and to your husband's life and work.

I remember an occasion shortly before the

marriage of my older sister when she was wrapped
up in all the planning and details of wedding
arrangements in which brides get enthralled. I am
sure there was no doubt in her mind about marrying
her fiance, and there was no objection to the
marriage by our parents, but I remember in the
midst of cleaning house one morning, Mother gave
her a final check (more like the third degree!). It was
done in love and for her welfare. Finally I heard
Mother say, "Well, now you be sure. Get it settled
once and for all, because there are not going to be
any divorces in this family!" Mother drilled it. "You
get it settled. You make up your mind. If he is the
right one for you, good, but if not, make it known
right now."

So Rebekah had her chance. She had the
decision to make. As an unmarried girl, you have to
make that decision whether you "will" or "will not"
according to God's will, because you have to live
with that decision the rest of your life. There is no
trial-and-error period in marriage. There is no
privilege of "Return for refund if not completely
satisfied!"

Commitment

Rebekah said, "I will go." She committed herself.
Genesis 2:24 says: "Therefore shall a man leave his
father and his mother, and shall cleave unto his
wife." God laid down that principle in the initial
pages of the Bible so that when you marry, your new
home becomes the nucleus. Rebekah had to make
her choice. She had to decide even against Mama in
this case. Her decision to marry didn't mean she
didn't love her mother. It didn't mean she would
never come back and see her mother as often as she

could, but she had to come to the point that if she was going to marry, her attention had to be to her husband and his work ahead of all other earthly things. Ruth spoke that classic verse that has come to mean so much at weddings. "Intreat me not to leave thee, or to return from following after thee: for whither thou goest, I will go; and where thou lodgest, I will lodge: thy people shall be my people, and thy God my God" (Ruth 1:16). That's how you must feel toward the man that God gives you.

Blessed is the mother who rears her daughter for that commitment. Don't rear your children for yourself. Don't rear them to keep them so close to the nest that when they get to the age when they are supposed to be thrust out into the harvest field for God they will be torn up inside because of the difficulty of leaving home. That doesn't mean you don't love them; it means that you are training them for the Lord. You ought to feel fulfilled inside when you see God's will being worked out in their lives, not crushed that they are leaving you.

One young Christian couple from Michigan had to face this problem. The young man had been called of God to go to the mission field. The girl loved him very much, she thought, until she received letters from her mother. Her mother put so much pressure on the girl that she simply was torn between the two. She wanted to go with the young missionary, but her mother was saying, "Oh, you don't want to go with him. You will go far away to the mission field, and you will be away from me. I might not see you for years at a time. Don't go with him." What a battle that girl had. Finally the young man felt he had been patient with her indecision long enough. So one evening when they were together, he took a little box out of his pocket, carefully opened the lid, and held before the girl he loved a simple, lovely diamond. One more time, perhaps for the last time for all he knew, he told her of his deep love for her. He told her he wanted her to be his wife and be with him always, but he said he knew God had called him to the mission field. He had to go. He had to obey God. He hoped, he deeply hoped she would marry him and go with him, but if she would not, he would have to go alone. In either case, he felt the matter had to be settled so they could move ahead for the Lord. He held the ring in one hand and his watch in the other and told her that he would give her two minutes to make up her mind. If she agreed to marry him, the ring would be hers; if not, they would have to part. He watched with terrible nervousness as the first minute ticked by. No answer. His heart nearly thumped out of his chest as the second hand ticked off the seconds of the next minute. The air was heavy with suspense and silence. Just when his hope was nearly gone, without even saying a word to him, she suddenly took the ring. With the decision made, what joy and assurance filled her heart. They have since fulfilled several terms on the mission field in Africa. They have one set of twins, and I don't know how many more children. No doubt they have had trials, but God has been faithful, and they have had a fruitful ministry doing His will. What a disaster it would have been if she had yielded to her mother's pressure. You have to do the Lord's will no matter what the cost. As a mother, rear your children to do the Lord's will. Prepare them for maturity. Put some life in their wings so they can rise from the nest to soar for God. God forbid that they should be forever grounded by the weight of a well-meaning but selfish home such as Jesus spoke of in Luke 9:61. When the young man there was called upon to follow the Lord, he could not make the break but put off discipleship with excuses: "Let me first go bid them farewell, which are at home at my house." "Me first," "at home," and "my house" ruled his heart rather than "Christ first" and "God's will."

Some parents are guilty of rearing dependent children. Such children get to be eighteen and twenty years of age and still depend on Mama. They have to run ask somebody about every little move. Now, I am not talking about sensible young folks seeking advice from godly people. I'm talking about kids who have to have Mom or Dad or someone do everything for them. They are almost useless for any profitable work. I know a girl who, when she went off to college, didn't even know how to wash her own stockings. I have known girls who got married and didn't know how to boil an egg, let alone cook or manage a home. Now, if the world wants to raise helpless little china dolls, that's their business, but Christian mothers had better be diligent from the time their girls are tall enough to stand on a chair and help wash dishes to train them for womanhood, to be keepers at home, to go to school with one thing in mind: to train every talent they have for the Lord. You don't know how the Lord may use your daughter. You don't know whether she will be a preacher's wife and end up having to do the bookkeeping and typing or keep the nursery or help sew for the needy and mission field or what or how she will be needed. She had better learn to sew and cook and type and take shorthand and whatever she can learn. She had better get all the training possible in music, too. Listen, if your children have a hair-breadth of talent in any area, get busy early training that talent as far as it can go. Don't take any talent or any ability as insignificant or unimportant. Search out the strengths and talents and get busy training them for the Lord.

A mother eagle is an amazing creature. She prepares with utmost care for the birth of her young by building a strong, secure nest of well-woven, long, sharp thorns, carefully covered and padded by her own feathers and down. She is very protective of and attentive to her young, but when those fledglings are mature enough to fend for themselves, the mother eagle does not have to push them out of the nest. She gradually removes the feathers and down from the nest until at last the remaining prickly thorns become so uncomfortable that the young eagles fly in spite of their love for their home-nest. Prepare your eaglettes to fly, to rise in the currents of God's wind, to resist the drag and weight of this world, to soar above the sin and selfishness of earth, and to be all they can be and do all they can do by the grace of Almighty God.

The morning after the celebration, Abraham's servant loaded the caravan and left for Lahairoi. Notice verse 61: "And Rebekah arose, and her damsels, and they rode upon the camels, and followed the man: and the servant took Rebekah, and went his way." I'm sure Rebekah took the personal clothing and supplies she and her damsels

needed for the trip, but she didn't spend days
sorting through everything and seeing what she
wanted to save from home. Another thing that
young marrieds need to get settled is this: when
God brings that special someone to your heart,
forget whomever you used to date and what you did
with him and where you went with him. I wouldn't
give a nickel for a girl who after she is married
throws former boyfriends up to her husband.
"Well," says she, "you know I used to go with so and
so. I could have married him." And she goes on
remembering how big and tall and handsome he was
and how much money he made. Do you know what I
would say if I were her husband? I'd say, "Get going,
Sugar! Hurry! Don't slow down! See if you can trace
him down and catch him!" because she wouldn't be
worth a nickel as a wife! If you knew or dated others
before you married, forget them. Burn their
pictures, letters, mementos, and don't ever bring
them up again. Burn the bridges behind you, and
don't resurrect past memories. Turn your heart and
devotion to the man whom the Lord has brought
you. Bring your devotion and love and energy and
kindness and loyalty to your marriage so that you
can give to him unselfishly your all.

You see, marriage isn't a fifty-fifty proposition.
Psychologists cooked that idea up to sound good
in magazine articles. No, ma'am! Marriage is not
a fifty-fifty proposition; it's a one hundred-one
hundred proposition. Both persons have to give one
hundred percent all the time. If you ever get up in
the morning and find yourself feeling selfish, then
you'd better get to the prayer closet right away and
ask God to help you get out of yourself that day. Be

honest with the Lord and pray, "Dear Lord, You know how bum I'm feeling. I'm getting in a mood. Lord, help me." A weakness of women is to get "in a mood." How we can make life miserable. We might not fuss; we just are silent. We "just don't feel like talking today." If you're sick, tell your husband so he doesn't wonder what in the world he did to upset you. The poor man thinks, "What did I do now to make her mad?"

Don't be as cold as a fence post or a refrigerator door; bring unselfishness, loyalty, love, warmth to your marriage every morning, every noon, every night. Make your husband glad to come home. Be there when he gets there. Have something he likes waiting for him to eat. Be ready to give your attention and time to him. A man can take a lot of stress from the outside world if at home he finds peace and quiet, love and warmth, support and loyalty. A two-room upstairs apartment over the back alley, a little white bungalow in the middle of a housing development, or a thatched-roofed hut in the muggy heat and dense growth of a tropical jungle can become the castle of a Christian man who is a servant of God. This phenomenon in great part is due to a warm, dedicated wife who sees her calling and work as one with her husband and whose heart is given to making him king of that castle.

Point of No Return

The night of much excitement and little rest passed quickly. The next morning the servant thanked the family for the fine hospitality and hurried to get the return trip underway. Rebekah's mother caught her breath and cried, "Oh! You didn't mean to take her this soon, did you? Why, this is too much of a shock!"

But the servant insisted, "Hinder me not, seeing the Lord hath prospered my way; send me away that I may go to my master."

Now in the next verse Miss Rebekah is put on the spot. They said, "We will call the damsel, and enquire at her mouth." Here is her chance to get out if she wants it. She hadn't been considered much up to this point as far as we know according to what is recorded in the Word, but now is her chance. It is a "speak now or forever hold your peace" situation. And so it is with young couples on the verge of marriage. Check it out well before you tie the knot. If your heart is not settled, if you don't know of a certainty that it is the Lord's will, if you are not absolutely sure, then back out. Do something! Don't tie the knot unless you are dead sure it is what you ought to do. The modern trend today is, "Well, we will go ahead and get married, and then if it doesn't work out, we can always get a divorce." The immoral Hollywood thrust in the nation is getting worse in that way all the time. It has gone so far now that if a couple is not sure they can make it in marriage, they try living together before they get married. Pitiful! Pitiful! That's not God's way! That's not the Bible way!

In verse 58, they asked Rebekah, "Wilt thou go with this man?" It seems she didn't hesitate. She didn't shift from foot to foot or wring her hands. She didn't cry, "What shall I do?" She simply said, "I'll go," and it was settled. Perhaps you think, "That crazy girl! She had heard about the guy only the day

before! How could she be that sure and settled
about it?" But Rebekah was no fool. She had seen
God's hand in the unfolding of the whole drama.
Anyway, she was depending on the Lord in the
matter. She hadn't been down at the well hunting a
boyfriend. She hadn't gone out to flirt to see if she
could lay a trap for a man. She had left the matter in
the Lord's hand altogether. She was busy doing
what her father had given her to do. She was busy
being where she was supposed to be at the right
time, and when the Lord opened the door, she was
ready. Her decision was based on a strong
foundation. It was not an emotional thing. Emotions
surely will be involved, but marriage has to be more
deeply based than that. She didn't argue with God's
will. All the providential events of the preceding
night pointed to one thing, and Rebekah was willing
to go with God's will.

She didn't coddle her mother's will. Her mother
was standing there begging her to stay a little longer.
"Just ten days," Mother insisted. "Why you know,
we have to get her trousseau together, and there is
some of Grandmother's best china I want to send
along. Oh, there is so much involved!" But Rebekah
said, "I'll go." She did not prolong the action when
she knew what was right to do.

It is easy even for Christian mothers to get in the
way of their children's doing the Lord's will. If God
blesses you with children, then don't rear them for
yourself. Don't try to keep them forever close.
Don't rear them so that you will have an absolute
nervous breakdown when they marry. That ought

to be a natural step in their lives according to the
Lord's will. You ought to feel fulfilled inside when
you see God's will being worked out in their lives,
not crushed that they are "leaving you." Why did
you bring them into the world? For yourself? To
coddle and baby them and make play-pretties for
you? To entertain you? No! God gave them to you
as His heritage to put into the mission field, into the
harvest field for Him, and you would be doing less
than your best for the Lord if you tried to hold them
forever to yourself and make them clinging vines.

Rebekah made the right decision. She was willing
to sail uncharted waters for the Lord. She said,
"Lord, I don't know what I'm getting into, but if this
is Your will, I'm willing. Yes, the servant says Isaac
has money, but that can disappear overnight." In
her heart, she had to settle "for richer, for poorer,
for better, for worse." Remember, she was going
four or five hundred miles away from home. She
could not catch the next plane out and fly back
home to Mama. She was leaving home perhaps
once and for all. She was leaving everything she
knew of security and comfort.

Discernment

Why was Rebekah willing to leave her home and
go to a life and land she knew nothing about? Well, I
think it was because she knew her man. You say,
"Why, she hadn't even seen the guy! How could she
possibly have known! What do you mean?" She was
leaving everyone she knew to go to a place she had
never been to marry a man she had never met, but
Rebekah's concern was the character of the man.
The character of the inner man was more important
than the countenance of the outward man. Her

family had sat up and listened most of the night
before while the servant represented the bride-
groom. How excited the servant was as he began to
tell about Isaac's miraculous birth. Isaac was a son
of promise, born far past the time that women bear
children. Rebekah knew that Isaac had been born
for a purpose, and now God was going to allow her
to be a part of that purpose. That must have thrilled
her heart.

She also knew Isaac was dedicated to the Lord.
He was not the kind who says, "Yes, I'm a Christian,
but I don't want the Lord to bother me concerning
my money or time or plans. I want to be saved and
go to heaven when I die, but the Lord should not
expect too much of me right now. I have things to
do, plans to fulfill, money to make, a business to
build, and pleasures to enjoy." That was not Isaac's
attitude. Rebekah knew that just as she had been
reared to obedience and self-discipline, so had
Isaac. She was sure of it because the servant told
about the time when Abraham made the journey to
sacrifice on Mount Moriah. He recalled the stop
halfway up the mountain when Abraham unloaded
the wood from the donkey and laid it on Isaac's
back. Perhaps the servant's voice caught in his
throat as he recounted Isaac's searching question to
his father, "Behold the fire and the wood: but where
is the lamb for a burnt-offering?"

Quietly Abraham replied, "God will provide
himself a lamb," and they kept walking. The two
continued to the top of that mountain, where Isaac
was willing to lay down his life in obedience to his
father because it was what God demanded. Isaac
was yielded one hundred percent to the will of God.

At that time he was a big, strapping teenager, and Abraham was an old man. Isaac could have run down the mountain and escaped from his father. He did not have to bow himself on that altar and allow his father to bind him. He could have fled. But when Abraham said, "God has commanded that you be the sacrifice, Isaac," Isaac's will was yielded to God's. Now when Rebekah learned that was the kind of man she was to marry, it made a great difference.

Rebekah also knew Isaac was a man of prayer and faith. The story in Genesis 24 later reveals that at evening he was out in the field meditating. No doubt this was a daily meeting with God. Isaac daily spent time praying and seeking God's will. Say, when you find that kind of man, you won't have to be scared of marrying him. And when you find that quality of man, do you really care what the outward "house" looks like? If a man is right on the inside, he will be neat and clean on the outside. He may not have the most expensive clothes but what clothing he has will look its best so he will be a testimony for the Lord. Rebekah was more concerned about the character of the man than she was about whether all the girls drooled when he walked by.

Many young ladies are looking for the wrong qualities in a man. All some girls care about is whether a boy is the most exciting, most popular man on campus. It doesn't matter to this kind of girl whether a man has integrity. It doesn't matter if he has character. It doesn't matter if he is honest. It doesn't matter if he would rather starve than steal. Nothing matters as long as he makes a splash in this world. But I tell you a man who makes a splash in this world won't last. He won't make a solid marriage that produces a happy home, that produces happy, dedicated Christian children yielded to the will of God. It is evident that Rebekah knew "what she was getting into," and it is no wonder she was willing to go. She hadn't seen Isaac, but she knew what a man he was.

Doesn't this remind you of the Scriptures as Peter speaks about the Lord Jesus Christ, "Whom having not seen, ye love"? You have never seen Jesus with your physical eyes, yet you know He loved you and you love Him. He laid down His life for you. He was completely dedicated to the Father's will. You haven't seen Him, but oh, you will not be disappointed! There's no disappointment in Jesus! When you see Him face to face, it will be more wonderful and more thrilling than your heart can imagine now. This is just a little shadow picture of the Lord Jesus Christ and His Bride.

Maturity

Rebekah was willing to go, because she knew her man. Now, young lady, if you are satisfied with a man of less caliber than Isaac, you will be disappointed. Of course, if you're a less caliber girl than Rebekah, then you'll be satisfied with a less caliber man. You see, it's a two-way street. While you are checking the man you're going to marry, you need to check yourself to see if you are as mature as you ought to be, because maturity is one of the most important ingredients in marriage. Just because a man or a woman has turned twenty-one doesn't mean that person is mature and ready for marriage. I have seen some people at fifty who never had grown up. I have seen some marriages go through very rocky times because the people involved were not as mature inwardly as their physical years indicated. They were regarded as adults by law, but they had never grown up on the inside. They were not ready to take responsibility. I knew one wife whose only thought at the grocery store was what she liked to eat. What her husband and children liked or needed was of no concern to her. All that mattered was what appealed to her and was easy to prepare. Do you call that maturity? I think not.

Maturity is also needed in control of personal habits. Paul said, "I keep under my body, and bring it into subjection" (I Cor. 9:27). A good sign of maturity is whether you are able to do what you ought to do, such as to eat what you ought to eat when you ought to eat and to leave off what you ought not to eat. I don't mean life must be made miserable, but you should be able to keep yourself under control. If you can't get out of bed on time before you're married because you know it's right to do, if you can't have devotions faithfully before you're married because you know you ought to, how in the world do you think you're going to do it after you're married? A man and woman ought to show maturity before they get married, because afterwards, it's going to be harder. Just saying "I do" doesn't make a person mature on the inside. A man who is twenty-one or so is not necessarily ready for marriage. He may still be slinging his clothes all over his room at home, unable to take the least responsibility. He may still be depending on his mother. You know, all some young men want is

another Mama. They do not want to be head of a
house. They do not want to take responsibility.
They just want somebody to mother them. Now
there are times when a man needs a little babying,
but don't marry a baby.

Honesty

Before marriage be sure both you and the man
you want to marry represent yourselves honestly.
This deserves serious consideration before marriage. Some people function beautifully in public but
cannot manage the quiet, daily routine of life in the
home. Some people seem to be the most talented
people in the world. They are the kind who are
elected "Man on Campus" or "Woman of the Year."
They seem to be everybody's friend, and in a crowd
they are the life of the party. They thrive on praise
and attention. But their marriage is a total disaster
because at home they are away from the glory, the
attention, the excitement, and the praise of the
crowd. At home, they cannot accept responsibility
that includes the humble routines of housework:
paying the bills, cutting the grass, and other
unglamorous chores that must be done in spite of
how they feel. A man's being a leader in public or the
life of the party does not necessarily mean he will
make a prize husband. Be sure the steady,
attractive man you know in public will be the same in
private after marriage.

A few years ago, we were invited to visit in the
parsonage of a church in a small town. I shall not tell
the name of the preacher or his wife. During dating
and courtship he had no doubt charmed her, but a
few years and two darling babies later, she was
broken and despondent. Oh, her husband was still

a preacher and had a church. From all outward appearances everything seemed fine, and even the folks in this church didn't appear to know what was taking place behind the scenes. The man simply would not take responsibility. He loved to play. I don't mean he was out with other women; he just loved to entertain himself and do what he wanted to do. If he wanted to go fishing, he went fishing. If he wanted to go politicking, he went politicking. And to save face before the church folks, guess who was writing his sermons on Sunday? You're right; his wife. He would get up on Sunday morning, lead the church service, and "preach" the sermon. He may have been a male, but he was not a man. He was nothing but a fake and fraud. Outside his home he was admirable, but at home he was a failure as a husband. I'm sure his wife spent many miserable, sleepless nights wishing she had discovered the truth about him before she had said, "I do." You say that is a grim warning. I say it is a very real and earnest warning. You had better make certain that the character of the young man who comes courting is indeed what it seems to be.

Helpfulness

When Rebekah climbed up on the camel and went with the servant, she turned her attention to the future, to making a life and home for her husband. When you marry that one man God gives you, from then on, he's the man on whom you concentrate. You need to think about this man that God gave you and be his helpmeet. That means you fill in what he needs. Wife, you ought to get up in the morning thinking about what he needs, what you can do to help him today rather than getting so wrapped up in what you have to do. What you have to do today, what you want to do, what your friends are going to do, or how your schedule is going to work out is not the most important. It's not your schedule or your career. Now I'm not against working women; I'd be in a fix if I were, for I've taught school and worked all of our married life. But I've heard women who chatter about, "My career, my career!" Hang your career! Your career is nothing. It's his career! What he's doing for the Lord and where you fit in to help him, that is the whole question. Anything you do as a wife is just to strengthen or enhance what your husband does for the Lord. That must be the purpose of our thought, our dedication to the job, the giving of our energy, our kindness, our loyalty, and our sacrifice. I know you have many things to do, but if you get things in the right order none of your responsibilities will suffer. If you put the Lord Jesus Christ first, then your husband will be in his right place. The children will be in their right place, and the house will somehow get taken care of if the Lord Jesus Christ is first in your home.

Under the Lord Jesus Christ your husband comes second, and you need to think about what you can do, what you can say that would help him. Have the coffee almost ready, so all you have to do is just set it out for him when he gets home in the evening. Save him a trip by running the errand yourself. Smile instead of frown. A sweet smile at the right time can mean more than money in the bank. Or just go through the house smiling instead of looking glum. He will suddenly think,

"Well, maybe things aren't so bad after all; she's smiling!" He may never say it aloud, but don't you worry, he's noticing, and it's making a difference right down deep in his heart. You can be a helpmeet in so many small ways.

Reward

At last Rebekah's journey was underway. What do you think Rebekah was thinking during all those days of travel? What fears could have welled up in her heart? But notice verse 63. (This is a great part of the secret of the success of this romance.) Isaac was meditating in the field at eventime. I am sure Isaac had diligently sought the Lord. "Oh, Lord, don't let the servant bring the wrong girl. Oh, Lord, let him bring the right one. Give me a wife who will be a help and a blessing and whom I can love. Oh, Lord, Thy will be done." Isaac's heart was assured by faith yet excited in hope and anticipation of the caravan's return.

Rebekah had been riding many days and many miles. Riding a camel is not like cruising in a Cadillac, so she must have been bone tired. But one evening she looked up and in the distance a man's figure was silhouetted against the horizon of the evening sky. She saw a man walking directly toward the caravan. Before introductions, their spirits met. I think in her heart she knew immediately who it was; she just wanted to hear it in words.

"Who is that walking to meet us?" she asked gently.

The servant answered, "It is my master."

Her heart fluttered, and her head spun in spite of the days of mental preparation for the moment, and then Rebekah took a veil and covered herself. Her

response was not to check her makeup. Her
response was not to try to make him understand
how fortunate he was that she had condescended to
be his bride. Her response was not to try to appear
sensual or seductive. "She took a veil and covered
herself." Her action speaks of modesty and respect
for the man who was to be her husband. It was a way
to show him that she was a virtuous woman, coming
gently, softly, and respectfully to let him take the
man's responsibility of bringing her to himself.

No doubt Isaac's heart filled with praise as the
servant recounted the events of the past few days
and told of the evidences of God's providential
leading. What joy must have flooded Isaac's soul as
he realized beyond any doubt that Rebekah was his
very own, handpicked in heaven. "And Isaac
brought her into his mother Sarah's tent, and took
Rebekah, and she became his wife; *and he loved
her.*" There's the story: *"And he loved her."*

What more could be said than "he loved her"?
What more could her heart desire than the
knowledge that "he loved her"? Yes, she knew he
was a rich man. Yes, she knew that everything his
father owned would someday be his. But all that was
nothing compared to the fact that "he loved her."
Drought could come and take away everything he
had. Windstorms could arise out of the desert and
blow away the tents and all the possessions they
counted valuable. Raiders could steal the cheeses,
the dried goat meat, and all the supplies that
assured security and prosperity for the next year.
But whatever might come, Rebekah was with Isaac,
"and he loved her." There is no better way for a
Christian girl to enter marriage. She should not ask,

"What's in it for me?" Rather she should say, "I will stand with my husband. He loves me, and I love him. By the grace of God we will do God's will and face whatever comes together."

As years passed, Rebekah's life was greatly blessed. Wealth abundant enriched her life. She became the grandmother of all the tribes of Israel and received honor and renown. But all of this was bound up in Isaac's love for her. However weak, however faltering, however inadequate she may have felt at times, he loved her. What a tender picture of the Lord Jesus Christ's love for you. What blessings, what riches, what gifts God has given you through His Son. If you started listing His blessings at sunrise this morning, you could not have half a list by sundown tonight. Yet with all those blessings and riches of His grace, the best is that He loves you. The Lord Jesus Christ loves you! He gave Himself for you, and if you are His by faith in His shed blood, someday you will see Him face to face; you will be with Him and enjoy His presence in heaven forever.

Question

Now, one question please. Who caught whom? Was Rebekah out trying to catch a man? Was she trying to see who was the town's most eligible bachelor and beat other girls to him? No, she didn't get Isaac by strategy and planning; she left the whole matter to God. She was faithful in her responsibilities, and God gave her a husband. Isaac was seeking her. And so can it be with you if you are faithful to the Lord. Put God's will first. Be sure you are willing to sacrifice your life to God's will no matter what the cost, and you won't have to catch a man. He will catch you! And when he does, he will know that he has a gem he can treasure forever. He will know the thrill of the truth of those verses in Proverbs: "Who can find a virtuous woman? for her price is far above rubies. The heart of her husband doth safely trust in her, so that he shall have no need of spoil. She will do him good and not evil all the days of her life."

Chapter 2

I Samuel 25: Abigail

There is an interesting story in I Samuel 25 about a lady named Abigail. "Abigail" seems like a rather unusual name, but it would be an honor for a girl to be named after this honorable woman. This story took place after Samuel died, and Israel was in a state of chaos. Israel had a king, Saul, but he had almost gone insane. A new king had been anointed, but he hadn't come to the throne yet, and there was strife between the two powers. I Samuel 25:1: "And Samuel died; and all the Israelites were gathered together, and lamented him, and buried him in his house at Ramah. And David arose, and went down to the wilderness of Paran." Now this was a time of real trouble in David's life. David had been anointed king, but since Saul had discovered what an honorable and strong person David was, Saul was jealous, insanely jealous. The daily desire of his heart was to find David and kill him. He had already tried to pin David to the wall with a javelin. But

by the mercy of God, David had darted out of the
way, and the javelin had stuck and hung quivering in
the wall. That had happened more than once. After
David left Saul's court, Saul sent his men out
hunting for David. This hunt had gone on for
months and months until David was nearly
exhausted. He lived not knowing when to stick his
head out from behind a tree because Saul's men
might be there to capture him. He was constantly
running for his life. During this time of pressure and
treachery this story takes place.

Verse two: "And there was a man in Maon,
whose possessions were in Carmel; and the man
was very great." "Great" means he was very
wealthy and powerful as far as the world is
concerned. Proof? He had a walking bank account.
Look at it. "He had three thousand sheep, and a
thousand goats." In that day, that was riches. Why,
he was self-sufficient. The milk from the goats
provided food for the family—milk, cheese, and
butter and such goods. The skins and wool
provided clothing for his household as well as
additional income from the wool and skins he sold.
Nabal was rich. But Nabal means "fool." He
certainly was well named. Nabal was a fool
twice—once because he thought that everything he
had was of his own doing. He thought his success
was due to "my brilliance, my ability in finance, my
ability in business, my knowledge of how to run this
ranch. I'm a self-made man. I earned it all.
Everything I have is mine. I control it, and I'm
number one." He was a fool again because he
rejected God, God's man, and God's message. Now
you can't be a greater fool than to think you're

bigger than Almighty God and reject His message of mercy and love.

Nabal was a fool. But look in the middle of verse three: "And the name of his wife was Abigail." What a contrast! "And she was a woman of good understanding, and of a beautiful countenance." Do you notice that God put the emphasis on the "good understanding" first? You see, it doesn't matter what you are on the outside. You could win the Miss America contest, but if you don't have good understanding and the right kind of heart, beauty won't keep your marriage together. Abigail was a woman of good understanding. The Scripture says, "If any of you lack wisdom, let him ask of God, that giveth to all men liberally, and upbraideth not." There will be many situations arising in your married life when you will say, "What shall I do? How shall I react?" Then ask the Lord for wisdom, and wait for it. Usually, we ruin the whole situation, and then we come back and say, "What should I have done, Lord?" We ought to seek the Lord first. Abigail had good understanding, and she was a beautiful lady.

"But the man was churlish and evil in his doings." There was not anything likable about the man. He was rough and proud. He was haughty, and nobody could do anything with him. He was an unreasonable man. And he was of the house of Caleb.

Diligence

Now, I want to depart at this point to make note of this man's heritage. Many generations earlier, Caleb was one of the twelve who was called to spy out the land of Canaan. He was faithful and was one of only two who brought back a good report. The heritage of Caleb was great. But apparently someone in the family line had failed to carry out God's injunction concerning training children. Israel had been instructed over and over to teach the Word of God diligently to the children, to show them God's hand and His work in history and in their heritage. Deuteronomy 6:7-9: "And thou shalt teach them diligently unto thy children, and shalt talk of them when thou sittest in thine house, and when thou walkest by the way, and when thou liest down, and when thou risest up. And thou shalt bind them for a sign upon thine hand, and they shall be as frontlets between thine eyes. And thou shalt write them upon the posts of thy house, and on thy gates." There wasn't anywhere they could go, anything they could do, or any place they could look without being reminded of God and of what He had done for them. And God said, "Keep it up. Don't let up." See Deuteronomy 11:18-20: "Therefore shall ye lay up these my words in your heart and in your soul, and bind them for a sign upon your hand, that they may be as frontlets between your eyes. And ye shall teach them your children, speaking of them when thou sittest in thine house, and when thou walkest by the way, when thou liest down, and when thou risest up. And thou shalt write them upon the doorposts of thine house, and upon thy gates." The purpose of keeping the commands of God before the children at all times was to create a desire to know and please God. That desire for knowledge would cause them to ask questions as in Deuteronomy 6:20: "What mean the testimonies, and the statutes, and the judgments, which the Lord our God hath commanded you?" Such questions opened the perfect opportunities to teach the children diligently.

Now I don't know who stopped teaching, I don't know who failed, but sometime down the generations in Caleb's line, somebody quit writing God's precepts on the doorposts and quit talking about them when they walked and when they sat and when they lay down. By the time the teaching reached Nabal's generation, there was no interest in God. So Nabal was just a proud fool, even though he had a better heritage than that. I'm saying that we as parents had better fear the Lord. We had better get down to business and teach His Word and His truth and what He's done for us. We should teach not only salvation but also the fear of the Lord day in and day out. You may take for granted that the children are getting the right instruction in school and in church and in devotions at home, but you had better take every opportunity to relate every little thing that happens to the Word of God so that there is nothing in the children's lives that they take for granted and so that they relate everything to the Lord. You may say, "Oh, my children will be all right. I talk to them all the time." Yes, but you don't know the fight of the devil. You don't know how intent he is on snatching them. You don't know how determined he is to have them and steal their faith and ruin their lives and make them of no effect for the Lord. You must fight daily to train your children for the Lord. Nabal had a wonderful heritage, but it had been lost before him.

Now we come to sheep-shearing time at Nabal's ranch. It's a time of work, but it's also a time of wonderful joy and celebration. They're eating well, they're drinking well. They're working long days but coming in at nights for a big feed. They're really celebrating! Why? The money crop is in, and it's the harvest and reward time of year. It's time to pick up paychecks. Nabal was celebrating.

Verses four—six: "And David heard in the wilderness that Nabal did shear his sheep. And David sent out ten young men, and David said unto the young men, Get you up to Carmel, and go to Nabal, and greet him in my name: And thus shall ye say to him that liveth in prosperity, Peace be both to thee, and peace be to thine house, and peace be unto all that thou hast."

David came with the right attitude. He didn't come haughtily expecting rewards, though he did know that out in the fields he had earned some. During the summer when the sheep were in the wilderness with the herdsmen, David had protected them. In all of his desperate running from Saul with his 600 men, he had helped protect Nabal's sheep. He had kept the wolves off at times. He had kept marauders out. If David had been a lesser man, he could have let the marauders come and then perhaps even have taken some meat for himself and his men who were half-starved. But rather than that, all during those long desolate months, David kept his men doing right, and if any trouble came up, they helped Nabal's herdsmen. They were a real blessing. One of Nabal's own herdsmen testified to that fact. Undoubtedly David had even talked with them about God and about what a wonderful friend He was and what He could do for them. A young man said to Abigail later, "We were conversant with them, when we were in the fields." David had had

the perfect chance to make havoc and slaughter to
get some good meat, but he hadn't done it. Instead,
he had protected Nabal's flocks. Now at harvest
time, he sent his men to say, "Look, we helped you.
We're hungry, and we would surely appreciate it if
you'd send us some meat. We have not harmed you,
and we surely would appreciate any provisions you
can give us."

Verse nine: "And when David's young men
came, they spake to Nabal according to all those
words in the name of David, and ceased." Look at
verse ten. Isn't this a shock? "And Nabal answered
David's servants, and said, Who is David? and who
is the son of Jesse?"

"Who is David?" Everybody in Israel knew who
David was. David was the one who had been
anointed king. David was Israel's hero. When Saul
and all the Israelites were in the war against the
Philistines, they all lay low in the trenches, scared to
stick their heads up for forty days. Then this young
man, David, appeared and said, "I'll take on the
giant." In a matter of a few minutes he stalked out
across the valley and in the name of the Lord said,
"Come on, giant! In the name of God I'm going to
take you for a trophy." The giant made terrible
mockery, you remember. He said, "Come on,
young'un, I'll feed you to the buzzards!" And David
answered, "No, I'm going to feed *you* and your
whole army to the buzzards!" And about that time a
stone flew from David's sling like a guided missile
and hit Goliath. He sank to the ground, never
knowing what hit him. Who was David? Indeed!
Everybody knew who David was. He was a hero.
His fame was so great that the women were saying,

"Saul has killed his thousands, but David his ten thousands!" The feats of David, his strength, his honor, and his bravery spread all over the country. Everybody knew who David was but Nabal. "Who is David?" he scorned. "Who is the son of Jesse? there be many servants now a days that break away every man from his master." Nabal put David in the category of a runaway slave, a renegade.

Notice Nabal's pride in verse 11: "Shall I take my bread, and my water, and my flesh that I have killed for my shearers, and give it unto men, whom I know not whence they be?" He used "I" or "my" seven times in one statement. Remember, he thought he was a self-made man. "I'm somebody," he thought. Proverbs 3:27 tells us, "Withhold not good from them to whom it is due, when it is in the power of thine hand to do it." In other words, if somebody is in need and there is something you can do about it, then get busy. Now David hadn't asked for anything unreasonable. In fact, David never should have had to ask. Nabal should have been sending out a company of men, saying, "Go find David, and reward him for his kindness and protection to us through this past summer." But now Nabal railed and raged, and sent David's men away empty-handed.

"So David's young men turned their way, and went again, and came and told him all those sayings."

Now there are two fires burning. "David said unto his men, Gird ye on every man his sword. And David also girded on his sword." You know whose sword he had, don't you? Goliath's! Now there are about 400 men streaming out across the wilderness, some on horses, all with swords, and David with the giant economy size! Nabal's smart-aleck message made David fume when his men came back and reported what Nabal had said. David was being hunted for his life. Every day his men were hungry, tired, and dirty. They were sleeping out under the open sky or in the caves or wherever they could. The tension at the camp was just like a tight cable ready to snap. And Nabal's message snapped the cable.

David left two hundred men at the camp to protect what they had and snapped orders to the remaining four hundred: "Men, get your swords. We're going! I'm going to take on a battle!" Say, you wouldn't have wanted to be in his path. He breathed, "I'm going to kill them all," and he intended to do just that. He said, "I'm going to ransack the whole place and burn it to the ground. There's not going to be anything left when I get done. I'm going to show Nabal who David is!" And David and his men tore out across the country to make a quick end to Nabal and all that he possessed.

Somehow one of Nabal's servants knew they were in for trouble so he hurried to tell Abigail. "But one of the young men told Abigail, Nabal's wife, saying, Behold, David sent messengers out of the wilderness to salute our master; and he railed on them. But the men were very good unto us, and we were not hurt, neither missed we any thing, as long as we were conversant with them, when we were in the fields: They were a wall unto us both by night and day, all the while we were with them keeping the sheep." He told the whole story. "And they're

coming, Miss Abigail, they're coming! You've got to
do something. They're going to kill us all!" Then he
urged, "Now therefore know and consider what
thou wilt do." That servant had pretty good sense.
He knew it would do no good to take his troubles to
Nabal. He went to Abigail, who was a woman of
good understanding. He said, "For evil is determined against our master, and against all his household: for he is such a son of Belial, that a man cannot
speak to him." The servant knew that Nabal was
totally unreasonable.

Communication

Not only did the servant know he wouldn't be
able to communicate the danger to Nabal, but
Abigail knew it too. I want to underline the
importance of communication in marriage. The
communication has to be kept going all the days of
your life. Do you really communicate with your
husband? Do you just tell him what you're going to
do today and quickly leave? Do you quickly say,
"I'm going to town. I'll see you later"? Or do you talk
things over? Do you keep him informed of your
activities and work? When you were dating, you
could talk things over together so well. You were
interested no matter what he was planning to do.
Even if you didn't care a thing about fishing, all of a
sudden fishing became your favorite subject. You
wanted to know all about the bait and the pole, and
you asked questions that were too dumb to ask, but
you were trying to show interest in what he was
doing. Right? But now he can do something big and
important, and you just don't take time to talk about
it. You just let him go on as if you didn't care. You
could ask, "What are you going to plant in the

garden this year?" But you think, "I know what he's going to plant. He planted Kentucky Wonders and Blue Lakes last year. I know what he's going to plant. Why bother to ask? Let him go do it." Hold it! Communication is everything. "Non-communication" can get started and build up unintentionally if you aren't careful. You can go on in silence not really intending to at all. You can just be irritated about something—something he said or did didn't strike you just right that morning, and in the afternoon he comes in from work with, "Hi, honey."

You're at the sink, and you don't answer.

"I'm home," he calls.

"Hello," you mutter.

"What'd you do today?"

"Nothing."

"Are you all right?"

"Yep."

"Anything wrong?"

"Nope." And under your breath you say, "I wouldn't tell you if there were."

You didn't really plan it that way. You didn't go through the motions of saying, "I'm going to give him the silent treatment. He's not going to get by treating me that way." But it happens. By that time he's on guard, so he goes on outside thinking, "If she's going to be that way, I'm just going on outdoors. She needn't think I'm going to stay around for that kind of treatment. Ornery thing! If she wants to be on silence, let her be on silence." Finally supper's ready, and you both sit down in silence. It's pretty miserable. Neither one is going to be the one to speak.

"If he thinks I'm going to apologize, he's got another think coming!" And the treatment goes on and the feeling rises, and a little something that wasn't anything becomes gigantic. Ephesians 4:26 says, "Let not the sun go down upon your wrath."

Bedtime comes. He gets on one side, turns his face toward the wall and his back toward you. You get on the other side, turn your face toward the wall and your back toward him, and never the twain shall meet.

"If he thinks I'm going to say 'Good night,' he can go jump overboard."

Finally he says, "Good night, honey."

"Good night." And there in the darkness two people are seething. Pretty soon, you start crying, but you'd die before you'd let him know it. You lie there and tears go down the pillow. Pretty soon you sob, just to let him know you're crying. I mean, what fun is it to cry if he doesn't even know it? What good does it do for you to be upset if he doesn't know you're upset? The darkness is heavy, and the silence deepens. There two people lie, hurt on the inside, and too proud to bend on the outside. But remember, "Let not the sun go down upon your wrath." Don't wait for him to be the one to speak first. Maybe he wasn't the one at fault to begin with. There's hardly a disagreement in which one person is totally wrong and the other is totally right.

The important thing is, don't wait for the other. Proverbs 15:1: "A soft answer turneth away wrath." Now it's not just soft vocally because you can say some things softly and still have a lot of bite. It's a soft, humble attitude that turneth away wrath. The mature person is the one who can say in the silent darkness, "Honey, are you awake?"

"Ummmm."

"I," and you can hardly get the words out, "Remember what I said this morning?"

"Yes."

"Well, . . . I surely am sorry."

After that first word, more than likely the other will say, "Oh, it wasn't you at all. It was me." And soon neither husband nor wife will allow it to be the other's fault, and then two lovers are arguing about who loves whom the most. Oh, don't be selfish, unwilling to come under and communicate and say, "I'm sorry."

What was Nabal's trouble? He was an unreasonable man, but the shoe can fit the female foot, too. Women can be unreasonable too. We can nit-pick. So we make a mountain out of a molehill. If we can just humble ourselves down and say, "Look, I'm surely sorry I said that. I know it was a misunderstanding," pretty soon the darkness will be light. The silence will be broken, and everything will be all right again, all because one was willing to be humble and give a soft answer of love and repentance and forgiveness, instead of saying, "I'm going to win this fight or else!" We go at a family disagreement like we were at a football game, determined not to let the opposition win. And who's the loser? You could win one argument and hurt your marriage for life. Now is it worth it? I say not!

Keep your communication system open in your marriage. It is easy for the sound system to go completely out and people be in silence, and that won't do. You have to have the sound system open

so you can communicate. You may have to swallow
your pride, you may have to swallow your tongue,
you may have to swallow some tears to talk, but so
many things can be worked out if you will keep the
communication lines open.

On the other hand, there is the danger of talking
too much. The Scripture says that the contentious
woman and the continual dropping on a rainy day
are alike. Too much talk can be just as bad as too
little if you are forever griping about problems.
"When are you going to fix that? When are you
going to fix that? When are you going to do this?"
You can be always complaining until he finally just
turns down his hearing aid. Husbands can do that,
you know. They can tune you out, because they
have heard and heard and heard you until they just
can't take any more.

The book of Proverbs has some key instructions
to the too-talkative wife. The advice found there
sometimes hurts. But it would pay every Christian
wife in blessed dividends to study, memorize, digest
the instructions of Proverbs. Don't ignore them.

Note Proverbs 16:32: "He that is slow to anger is
better than the mighty; and he that ruleth his spirit
than he that taketh a city." How many problems at
home could be averted if you would just hold your
tongue, think before you speak, simmer down
before you spout.

Proverbs 17:14: "The beginning of strife is as
when one letteth out water." Watch out when that
feeling rises, and you feel compelled to say how you
feel about things. You don't intend to start an
argument, but you're going to have your say. But
speaking your piece one more time opens the crack

in the dam that starts the water spewing and takes much time and repair work to stop. "Therefore leave off contention, before it be meddled with." Don't make an issue of something that is not important. Let the little things go by. Save your words for times when something vital is at stake.

Here's another reason to keep the communication lines open. Proverbs 20:18: "Every purpose is established by counsel: and with good advice make war." Get your family forces together rather than fighting each other. Counsel together. Talk things out.

Proverbs 15:1: "A soft answer turneth away wrath." There are times when one of you comes home angry, and all it takes is two to make an argument. If your husband is filled with wrath or irritation, a soft answer can turn the tide. Sometimes he only needs a sounding board, a listener. You don't have to respond or speak your mind on every issue. "A soft answer turneth away wrath."

Proverbs 21:19 is a jewel. "It is better to dwell in the wilderness, than with a contentious and an angry woman." Now remember that the next time your "Irish" gets stirred up. Your husband would be better off living out in the desert if you are going to cause a commotion around the house.

Proverbs 15:17 is a favorite. "Better is a dinner of herbs where love is, than a stalled ox and hatred therewith." It's better to have turnip greens and cornbread or field peas and water biscuits for supper if you sit down to the table with love and harmony in your hearts and gratitude to the Lord for the supply of your needs rather than to be eating

U.S. prime beefsteaks in an atmosphere of harsh words and cold feelings. Whatever fancy fare you may have somehow won't taste very good unless there's love and harmony at the table. Yet, you can make it through some tough times eating bare minimums, meager fare can taste mighty good, and you can enjoy it and thank the Lord for it when things are right at home.

Proverbs 25:11: "A word fitly spoken is like apples of gold in pictures of silver." What a picturesque verse. What a challenge for a good wife, who is constantly looking out for her husband, watching for his needs, watching for his problems, having her ears and eyes alert for what would help him. Sometimes just the right word at the right time can be such an encouragement to his heart. You know when you get riled you may think, "I wish I were a man. I would tell you what I would do." And then when you are yourself again you think, "Am I glad I'm not a man! What would I do with all the responsibility?" Your husband has burdens that you don't really realize. He may come home from work having had pressures during the day that you know nothing about, yet you stand ready to load him down with every difficulty that you have had at home all day. Give him time. Feel your way; don't burden him. "A word fitly spoken" is such a blessing at the right time. Be an encourager. Watch your tongue with the one you love most. The ones who mean the most and are dearest to you usually end up being the ones who catch the sharpest cutting edge of your tongue. You're with them day and night in every kind of situation. You're with the people at work only during work hours. You make appointments to be with friends. And you're careful to be polite and gracious to workers and friends when you are with them. If we could only be as concerned and careful about the feelings of our husband and family as we are about those people we see only once a week, what a difference it would make. We need to be careful and concerned about the feelings of the ones who mean most to us, because they are the ones God has given us to labor together with in His service.

I would recommend to you the reading of James 3 often. Read it again and again, asking the Lord to help you remember the truths of this chapter. The illustration in verse 3 is rather humorous. "Behold, we put bits in the horses' mouths, that they may obey us; and we turn about their whole body." You can control the will of a powerful horse with a good bit in his mouth. James also says you can take a great ship out in the fiercest wind, and with just a very small helm, you can control that big ship. But a tongue, small as it is, is next to impossible to control. Verses 5-6a: "The tongue is a little member, and boasteth great things. Behold, how great a matter a little fire kindleth! And the tongue is a fire, a world of iniquity." More trouble is caused in homes by sharp words or by something said without discretion. Oh, how much trouble could be averted just by controlling the tongue.

Verses 8-9a: "The tongue can no man tame; it is an unruly evil, full of deadly poison. Therewith bless we God, even the Father; and therewith curse we men." Oh, we can pray and praise the Lord and sound spiritual and then turn right around and with the same tongue tell somebody off. James says,

"Brethren, these things ought not so to be."

Now verse 13: "Who is a wise man and endued with knowledge among you? let him shew out of a good conversation his works with meekness of wisdom." In her meekness, humility, and good understanding, Abigail used her tongue wisely. If anybody had reason to be upset, Abigail did, yet we will see she knew how to control herself. "This wisdom descendeth not from above, but is earthly, sensual, devilish." And that's the spirit we show when we lose our temper. You say, "But I'm a Christian." Yes, but we Christians can lose control and say things we regret later. Afterwards we say, "Oh, I didn't mean to say that." But the damage is done. This happens when we have sidestepped the Lord, and have climbed into the driver's seat instead of letting the Holy Spirit have full control. We have been earthly and sensual and devilish.

Verse 17: "The wisdom that is from above is first pure, then peaceable, gentle, and easy to be intreated." A person ought to be reasonable. "Full of mercy and good fruits, without partiality, and without hypocrisy." We talk about hypocrites in the church, but we can be hypocrites at home, too. We say one thing while doing and feeling another way inside. Study James 3. It's an important chapter for any Christian, but especially for Christian women.

Self-Control

Now let's resume Abigail's terrible circumstance. There is David, furious and coming with his men, some on horses and some on foot. They're ready to burn Nabal's place down. Then there is Nabal who has shown himself to be the fool that his name indicated. Abigail is in a precarious place. The

Scripture says that she is a woman of good understanding, so it's worth finding out what she's going to do. This is what I call "crisis control." It's what you do in a crisis that shows what you really are. Every day in marriage is not going to be easy. Every day isn't going to be Honeymoon Haven; some days are going to be Household Hassle. Some days are going to be problems, problems, problems. Some of the problems will be little, and some will be so big you wish you could get under the bed and stay there. Some will be money matters, some will be sickness, sorrow, and even death. Life is full of problems. There will be little ones, such as the bread didn't rise and dinner company is already at the door. What are you going to do? Are you going to have a nervous breakdown and make the company wish they never had even been invited, or are you going to handle it? Then there are the big serious things when a real crisis comes. Dr. Bob Jones, Sr. used to say: "A crisis doesn't make or break a man. A crisis reveals what he was all the time." It's easy to live calmly when things are going well, but a crisis reveals what you really are.

This crisis revealed Abigail. What are the possible responses in a situation like this? You can become angry and snap at whoever caused the problem and at people who are no part of the problem simply because you are frustrated. You can be contentious and quick-tempered. You have seen some women like that. You dread their anger. They are unreasonable. They tell you off and perhaps glory a little in their ability to do so. And if you dread their anger, how do you think their husbands must feel? Another possible response in a crisis is to simply "go to pieces" and cry. Then somebody else will have to do something. They can't just watch a lady cry. You can put the whole load on your husband's shoulders and cry and carry on without any self-control. Or, you can wait on the Lord.

There are some things in life about which you can get angry, and it won't do any good. You may cry and get upset, but it won't help the situation. You can sit and sulk, you can get mad at yourself, you can get mad at your husband, you can get mad at anybody you want to but it's not going to do any good. As you carefully think the problem through, if, as far as you know, there's nothing you can do, there's no use to make yourself and everybody else miserable. There's a time when you just have to be still and wait on the Lord and let Him work.

Proverbs 20:22: "Say not thou, I will recompense evil; but wait on the Lord, and he shall save thee." That's right. There are times when there's no getting even. All you can do is wait on the Lord.

Psalm 27:14: "Wait on the Lord: be of good courage, and he shall strengthen thine heart: wait, I say, on the Lord." Twice in one verse it says, "Wait." Wait; don't get discouraged. Listen, when a crisis comes, the devil will jump on you to try to get you so discouraged that you wish you could die. Right? Some of you have had such an experience. You have to take the promises of the Word of God, get a grip on yourself by the grace of God, and just say, "Well, Lord, I'm waiting on You. There's nothing I can do; I leave the matter in Your hands." And then don't fret and worry.

Psalm 37:34: "Wait on the Lord, and keep his

way, and he shall exalt thee to inherit the land: when the wicked are cut off, thou shalt see it." Some problems can't be handled overnight. Some things take time and you have to wait and let the Lord work. Let Him do the exalting at the right time.

Isaiah 40:31: "But they that wait upon the Lord shall renew their strength; they shall mount up with wings as eagles; they shall run, and not be weary; and they shall walk, and not faint." How do you like that promise? Isn't that great? When everything looks bleak and dark, cling to this verse. Wait on the Lord. The Lord gives strength to keep on keeping on even when you think you can't.

Job 13:15: "Though he slay me, yet will I trust in him: but I will maintain mine own ways before him." No matter how black the sky gets, don't let your faith be shaken. You have to be careful, or you will say, "Why would God do this to me? Why, why, why?" You can start asking questions and get out of focus with the Lord. You have to settle it and say, "It doesn't matter what happens, I'm going to trust Him." Romans 8:28 says, "All things work together for good to them that love God, to them who are the called according to his purpose." Now if God's Word is right (and it is), then I've got to believe it, and I can't get veered away from it. You have to anchor to the Word of God!

Proverbs 3:5-6: "Trust in the Lord with all thine heart; and lean not unto thine own understanding. In all thy ways acknowledge him, and he shall direct thy paths." Wait and trust, and trust and keep on waiting, and keep on trusting. Now that's not easy to do. Sometime you may think, "I can't stand it. I'm going to have to do something!" So you run out and do the wrong thing. Dr. Bob Jones, Sr. used to say, "Don't do anything until you know what to do"; otherwise, you will run ahead of the Lord. You will do something that will backfire, and you will be in worse trouble than you were before. Now, don't run ahead and do something if you don't know what is right to do. Wait on the Lord.

This passage is a jewel. Isaiah 26:3-4: "Thou wilt keep him in perfect peace, whose mind is stayed on thee: because he trusteth in thee. Trust ye in the Lord for ever: for in the Lord Jehovah is everlasting strength." That's an anchor for times of trouble and stress. He will keep you in perfect peace if your mind is stayed on Him. But mark this down, if you don't stay in the Word, in a time of trouble and crisis you will lose your stability. The Lord has to do it. He has to move the mountains. He may also have to move men, but He must do it, and all you can do is pray and trust and wait.

There are other times when you have to handle a matter. You can't wait until your husband comes home to take care of it. You can't wait for something to work out. You have to make a decision and act on it. Those times take courage. You have to do what you can do. It may not be what somebody else would do who was smarter or richer or greater or stronger, but it's what you can do when God puts the problem in front of you. I imagine you can look back and remember a time or crisis when something your mother did or said changed a whole situation, when her calmness kept everyone level.

Clementine Paddleford in *A Flower for My Mother* tells of her mother's strength, stability, and common sense. She relates a time when her family lived out on the Kansas plains and the house caught on fire. Her mother said, "Clemmie, run to the timber, and tell Papa the house is on fire. Tell him not to worry. Mother will take care of it." So there goes Clemmie hopping and skipping out to the timber. She no more got the words "house on fire" out of her mouth than the men were running like fury to get to the fire. But it hadn't worried Clemmie. Her mother had said she would take care of it, and Clemmie knew she would. And she did. She climbed up and chopped a hole in the ceiling, and let the smoke out; then she gave the general ring on the telephone and all the neighbors came to help. Her mother had said, "Don't worry," so Clemmie hadn't worried. Mother had it all under control.

She also told of a lesser crisis that would have been major to many women. On Clemmie's tenth birthday, she was to have a big birthday party. Her mother had invited the children from the surrounding area. The farms were scattered, so some children had come many miles. Mother had invited the children to come and play games in the afternoon, and then she was to have early supper for them. Mother had fixed up the dining room table with a crepe paper cloth with some home-grown summer flowers in the center. Mother had fried chicken and mashed potatoes. Country cooking was much work, but it was so good and seemed so wonderful to a child. At last her mother opened the dining room door for her to come in to see the table and discuss the seating of the guests. When Clemmie saw the dining room, the sight just took her breath away—that pretty pink crepe table cloth, and the flowers, and the food, and all of it all together was just too much. She hadn't seen anything so beautiful in all her life. In her excitement she planted her hands on the sofa beside the table, gave a squeal of joy, and kicked up her heels. Well, that kick knocked the extra boards out of the table and potatoes, gravy, flowers, and chicken went all over the floor. Clemmie stood frozen. You can imagine how her mother must have felt after all those hours of preparation. But she merely said, "Clemmie, you are not to cry. You are ten years old, and you are not to cry. I will get supper again." She shooed the children out. Big sister had to think up more games for another couple of hours. Big brother had to go out and kill more chickens and dress them. Mother started over from scratch and cooked supper again. Miss Paddleford said, "When supper was ready again, it was about the hungriest mob for a birthday party you ever saw." When they opened the dining room doors this time, there was Mother's best linen table cloth that she had thought was too good for the little children to eat on the first time, and there was the best china, and the best of everything. There were fresh fried chicken and mashed potatoes. Mother had taken care of it rather than have everything ruined for Clemmie's birthday. It was not a great crisis, but it was a crisis in the child's life, and Mother took care of it.

Now there are big crises at your house and there are little ones, but how you handle them makes all the difference. I remember in the summer of 1948 when we had a terrible tornado. The storm came suddenly. The men tried to get to the house, but some never made it. The wind was so strong that the rain came through the sides of the walls. At first Mother and Dad tried to put buckets around to catch the water, but it was no use. They were concerned about where different men were and if they were safe, but I don't remember being frightened. The huge sixty-foot silo was smashed to the ground like powder and the iron girders were twisted like hair ribbons. The big threshing machine was turned over like a tin can. The big, white, two-story barn that had stood for over half a century was blown away. But through all the storm I don't remember that anybody went to pieces. I don't remember hearing my parents even mention insurance. They were the Lord's, and somehow God would see them through. Now that's the kind of stability children need. Don't disintegrate when crises come. If we believe God's Word, then we must cling to it and act accordingly. "And we know that all things work together for good to them that love God, to them who are the called according to his purpose." All right then, walk tall. Meet the crisis in the name and power of the Lord. Cling to His promises, and don't let the crisis shake your faith. Proverbs 16:20 is a good verse to remember when a crisis comes, whether it is the bread falling flat or the pie getting turned over and ruining the rug or the children getting muddy just at the time to leave for church. Whatever the problem, remember Proverbs 16:20: "He that handleth a matter wisely shall find good: and whoso trusteth in the Lord, happy is he." Handle a matter wisely. Ask the Lord for wisdom. I think the word discretion is the key to a woman's life. Proverbs 19:11: "The discretion of a man deferreth his anger; and it is his glory to pass over a transgression."

Proverbs 24:10: "If thou faint in the day of adversity, thy strength is small." Does that verse ever upset you? Just about the time you think you are ready to give up and say, "Phooey on the whole mess. It's just not worth the trouble," then that verse comes in loud and clear. "If thou faint in the day of adversity, thy strength is small." Your strength is to be the Lord. It would be a reflection on the Lord and a reproach to His name to quit. Proverbs 15:33: "The fear of the Lord is the instruction of wisdom; and before honour is humility." And then Proverbs 24:3: "Through wisdom is an house builded; and by understanding it is established." Wisdom and understanding we need. And then a key, Proverbs 31:17: "She girdeth her loins with strength, and strengtheneth her arms." Simply rise to the occasion. "The house is on fire!" "Mother will take care of it." "You are not to cry. Mother will take care of it." By the grace of God, you will stand. You will do it. You won't shrink from responsibility or opportunity. Do what you can do. Be a resourceful person. If your husband is there, follow his leadership. But there will be times when you have to rise to the occasion yourself. Be calm. Call on the grace of God, and do what you can do.

Now Abigail could have gone to Nabal and said, "Look what a mess you got us into now. If you think I'm going to sit by and watch, you're wrong." She could have stormed at him, but what good would it have done? It would have probably caused a battle. Nabal might have risen up and said, "I'll show you what I can do," and gathered his men and headed out to fight David. They would have had an awful battle, and the field would have been full of dead men.

Abigail could have cried and played helpless, but that probably would have prompted the same response, or Nabal might have shoved her aside and said, "I can't abide a bawling woman." All such a response would have done would be to make him madder.

Abigail couldn't talk to Nabal because he was an unreasonable man. So, as Proverbs 31 says, she strengthened herself. She took two hundred loaves, two bottles of wine, five dressed sheep, five measures of parched corn, two hundred clusters of raisins, and two hundred cakes of figs and laid them on asses. Let me tell you, that was a job. I know she had servants to help, but somebody had to organize all the work. Two hundred loaves of bread. Have you ever baked bread? I consider three big loaves a job. Abigail had two hundred going. Abigail had to direct the preparation without disturbing Nabal and causing a furor. They baked bread and butchered, cooked, and prepared five sheep. I don't know whether she barbecued them or had lamb chops or leg o' lamb, but she got five of them ready to take to David. When everything was prepared, Abigail had it all loaded on the donkeys ready to go. Then she led the caravan to meet David. This was no task for a delicate, helpless woman; it was a challenge for a godly woman who strengthened herself, because her life and household were at stake.

Abigail had a crisis on her hands, but that crisis revealed her faith and her timber. She put herself under some hardship to meet the situation. After that servant had come and warned her about the danger, she had to have great bravery to head out across that wilderness to meet David as angry as he was. She didn't know but that she would be murdered and left in the desert. But she took the risk in order to save her household and her husband, and, we will see later, David himself. And so "she came down by the covert of the hill, and, behold, David and his men came down against her." David was fuming. He had said earlier: "Surely in vain have I kept all that this fellow hath in the wilderness so that nothing was missed of all that pertained unto him: and he hath requited me evil for good" (I Sam. 25:21). And then he had made the promise, "I'll wish worse on me if I don't get rid of him and all his family and everything that he owns by this time tomorrow." David intended to go down there and bring the whole ranch to dust and rubble in revenge for Nabal's evil treatment, and David came thundering across the hills. What do you think Abigail thought when she looked up and in the distance saw a cloud of dust rising toward the sky and realized it was David and his army?

When Abigail saw David and his men, she might have thought, "Lord, what have I done? What have I got myself into?" Her heart must have been filled with prayer that the Lord would make the situation work out for His honor and glory. Once again Abigail showed good understanding and wisdom. Verses 23-24 tell what she did: "When Abigail saw David, she hasted, and lighted off the ass, and fell before David on her face, and bowed herself to the ground, And fell at his feet, and said, Upon me, my lord, upon me let this iniquity be." Her first words

were of humility and sacrifice. She had not been at
fault in any way, but she was taking the blame for the
whole problem before David in order to spare his
name, his reputation, and her husband's life and
property. She laid herself on the ground before him
and humbly took the responsibility for the whole
matter. "Let thine handmaid, I pray thee, speak in
thine audience, and hear the words of thine
handmaid. Let not my lord, I pray thee, regard this
man of Belial, even Nabal: for as his name is, so is he;
Nabal is his name, and folly is with him."

You remember "Nabal" means "fool." He had
shown his foolishness by his outward actions. "But I
thine handmaid saw not the young men of my lord,
whom thou didst send." She said, "I don't know
anything about Nabal's mistreating your men, but
as soon as I found out about it, I came to see you."
"Now therefore, my lord, as the Lord liveth, and as
thy soul liveth, seeing the Lord hath withholden thee
from coming to shed blood, and from avenging
thyself with thine own hand, now let thine enemies,
and they that seek evil to my lord, be as Nabal. And
now this blessing which thine handmaid hath
brought unto my lord, let it even be given unto the
young men that follow my lord. I pray thee, forgive
the trespass of thine handmaid: for the Lord will
certainly make my lord a sure house; because my
lord fighteth the battles of the Lord." Her faith came
through! Nabal didn't care who David was, but
Abigail knew who he was, and she knew the
testimony of David. She said, "God's going to see
you through, because you're fighting for the Lord."
Notice the insight she had. "Yet a man is risen to
pursue thee, and to seek thy soul." She knew about

Saul's treachery and that Saul was hunting David. She knew that David had been living in the caves and in the woods. She said, "But the soul of my lord shall be bound in the bundle of life with the Lord thy God." She assured David that God was going to protect him. "And the souls of thine enemies, them shall he sling out, as out of the middle of a sling." She had heard about David's killing Goliath, and she assured David that his enemies were going to be destroyed with terrible force, as a rock out of a sling. What an encouragement she must have been to him that day. What a surprise for David to hear such wisdom and encouragement about God's protection and victory. "And it shall come to pass, when the Lord shall have done to my lord according to all the good that he hath spoken concerning thee, and shall have appointed thee ruler over Israel"—she even knew he was coming to the throne—"that this shall be no grief unto thee, or offence of heart unto my lord, either that thou hast shed blood causeless, or that my lord hath avenged himself." In other words, she said, "You're going to come to the throne one day, and you're not going to want to look back and feel guilty for what you did in a flare of temper. You're not going to want a massacre on your conscience."

And now notice her crowning plea: "But when the Lord shall have dealt well with my lord, then remember thine handmaid." What eyes of faith! David didn't any more look like a king out there in the wilderness than a jackrabbit. He had been roughing it. He looked as much like a king as the donkey on which she was riding. He had been sleeping out under the trees at night with the dew in his hair. I expect the only place he had to bathe was in the streams when he could get time running from Saul. He and his men had to cook over an open fire. He probably smelled like smoke and was covered with dust. He was the least likely example of a king, but she looked right past all that and knew what God had promised David. And she said, "When you come to your throne, remember me."

Doesn't that remind you of the thief on the cross? He looked over and saw the Lord Jesus Christ hanging naked on the cross, emaciated, torn, and covered with blood. But he looked past all that and saw a glorified body clothed in robes of righteousness. He saw that terrible crown of thorns that punctured Jesus' brow and somehow with eyes of faith it spun into a royal diadem. He saw that cross on which Jesus hung, and somehow eyes of faith turned it into the throne of God, the judgment seat of Christ, and he saw Jesus high and lifted up. And he said, "Lord, remember me when Thou comest into Thy kingdom."

So this is a beautiful picture of salvation when Abigail saw in David not just a man running for his life, not just a bold soldier fighting battles, but looking past all that she saw a king on a throne.

After charging across the country ready to kill anything in his path, David stood there and listened to Abigail as she bowed in the dust. I have no doubt that there were tears streaming down her face as she pleaded and reasoned with David and tried to make him see that he was not only hurting Nabal but that he was hurting himself and his own testimony. Strange as it may seem, suddenly those muscles that had been so taut and tight, those eyes that had been so sharp and piercing and ready to dart at anything, those shoulders that had been so straight and tense began to relax as she knelt before him. And it wasn't long before that warrior who had been so strict and stern bent over and gently lifted Abigail up out of the dust and helped her to her feet. (That is just what Jesus Christ will do for you when you come humbly to Him for mercy and forgiveness of sin. By the power of His precious blood, He lifts you up out of the dust and degradation of sin and stands you firm on His foundation.) And the voice that had been so gruff with threats of revenge now spoke tenderly, "Blessed be the Lord God of Israel, which sent thee this day to meet me." First he praised the Lord; then he praised her: "Blessed be thy advice." (Say, did you ever hear a man thanking a woman for her advice? You'd better frame this verse!) "Blessed be thy advice, and blessed be thou, which hast kept me this day from coming to shed blood, and from avenging myself with mine own hand. . . . So David received of her hand that which she had brought him, and said unto her, Go up in peace to thine house; see, I have hearkened to thy voice, and have accepted thy person."

Peace

Oh, she was a peacemaker, wasn't she? And that's what Jesus is to us. He puts our hand in God's hand and becomes the connecting link, and God says, "I've hearkened to the voice of the Son of God." We don't deserve anything, but we come to the Lord Jesus Christ and God receives us through Him. It's wonderful! What a wonderful joy it must have been to Abigail's heart that day as she and all the servants began to unload all the meat and bread and fruit and other supplies and took them over to David and his men.

Abigail must have watched for a long time as David and his men started back over the hills to their camp. What a wonderful thing God had done for them that day. What a wonderful victory. He had spared her life, and her husband's life, and the whole household. Why, it was a wonder she didn't run that donkey's little legs off trying to get home to tell Nabal what wonderful things God had done for her that day.

But her homecoming was sad. Verse 36 says: "And Abigail came to Nabal; and, behold, he held a feast in his house, like the feast of a king; and Nabal's heart was merry within him, for he was very drunken: wherefore she told him nothing, less or more, until the morning light."

Unequal Yoke

I don't know how Abigail got into this marriage. I've often wondered. Maybe she was a victim of an oriental child-marriage in which the parents give the children away in marriage contracts while the children are little more than babes. Perhaps she had to marry the highest bidder. Or perhaps she didn't put her faith and trust in the God of Israel until she was older, and somehow in her early days, living for self, she married this man. Maybe when she married, neither of them was saved; then afterwards, she trusted the Lord of Israel. I don't know how it happened, but I know she was in a miserable situation.

Let this be a warning to you never to marry someone who is not saved. The marriage will not work. There's no fellowship. Abigail needed someone to confide in. Her heart was so full; she had so much to share, and there was no one with whom to talk. She wanted to tell Nabal so much, to talk to him, to share the whole experience with him, but there he was, *drunk!* What would he understand? Nothing. There was no bond of love between them. There was no basis for fellowship. There was no understanding in that godless person. There was nothing for her to do but to slip by him as quietly as possible and spend the night by herself. No doubt she spent much time in prayer thanking the Lord for His mercy, but I don't doubt that there were tears of loneliness and sorrow too. Sometimes her heart must have cried, "Oh, God, if only my husband knew Thee!"

A husband and wife need to be in perfect harmony, but if both are not Christians, there's no way the harmony can be complete. Oh, the heartache that is ahead when a young girl says, "Oh, I know he's not saved, but I'll be a good testimony, and he will get saved after we get married." Don't bank on it! When you go into a marriage willingly knowing you are doing wrong, you're asking for trouble. Weddings are beautiful, but the bouquets don't last long if both the husband and wife are not right with God and both are not wanting God's will completely.

II Corinthians 6:14-15: "Be ye not unequally yoked together with unbelievers: for what fellowship hath righteousness with unrighteousness? and what communion hath light with darkness? And what concord hath Christ with Belial? or what part hath he that believeth with an infidel?" Nabal and

Abigail are the perfect example of the unequal yoke. What a warning this story ought to be to young lovers! Abigail went back home, but her night was lonely and destitute even though God had done wonderful things for her that day, because there was no concord, no fellowship, no communion. She had to slip by her drunken husband hoping he wouldn't notice her and lash out.

Recompense

Alone in the darkness, the night must have seemed like an eternity to Abigail. Of course, it was nothing to the crude Nabal.

He knew nothing about it until morning. Verse 37: "But it came to pass in the morning, when the wine was gone out of Nabal, and his wife had told him these things, that his heart died within him, and he became as stone." Without warning he was struck down. The shock of the close call he had had was more than his inebriated heart could stand. Judgment fell quickly. The Scripture says, "He became as stone." He lay in a coma for about ten days, but he apparently never regained consciousness. Nabal had passed his opportunities for repentance. "And it came to pass about ten days after, that the Lord smote Nabal, and he died." He had no more chance of repentance.

Proverbs 29:1: "He, that being often reproved hardeneth his neck, shall suddenly be destroyed, and that without remedy." Nabal is proof of this verse. Nabal had mocked and scorned God's servant. He considered himself a self-made man responsible to no one. God is long-suffering, not willing that any should perish, but when people blatantly scoff Him and choose their own way, they stand in mortal danger. "He, that being often reproved hardeneth his neck, shall suddenly be destroyed, and that without remedy." God just finally pulled down the shade and said, "This is it, Nabal: you've had your last chance." "For he saith, I have heard thee in a time accepted, and in the day of salvation have I succoured thee; . . . behold; now is the day of salvation" (II Corinthians 6:2). That's the urgency of salvation. Don't put it off! Don't think that when you make your first million, then you will get right with God; when you get all your problems straightened out, then you will get right with the Lord; when you get the children reared, then you will get right. No, my dear, don't put it off. "Behold, now is the accepted time, now is the day of salvation." Nabal had been boasting all that week, but now Nabal's chances were over. The breath he had used to curse God and mock God's servants was gone. Suddenly he stood horribly alone, stripped of his pride and self-esteem, utterly destitute and unprepared to face a holy God.

I don't know what kind of funeral they had for Nabal, but when David heard that Nabal was dead, he said, "Blessed be the Lord." Now he wasn't thankful that Nabal was dead for Nabal's sake, but it reminded him once more of God's mercy in keeping him from killing Nabal and having Nabal's blood on his hands. We don't know how many times God keeps us from making costly, deadly mistakes. David thanked the Lord: "Blessed be the Lord, that hath pleaded the cause of my reproach from the hand of Nabal, and hath kept his servant from evil."

God says, "Vengeance is mine." Here is a principle that we as Christian women need to get settled. It's easy to get upset when your husband is mistreated or you are slandered or someone tries to hurt you. You want to fight back, but here's the verse: "Dearly beloved, avenge not yourselves, but rather give place unto wrath: for it is written, Vengeance is mine; I will repay, saith the Lord" (Rom. 12:19). If there's any avenging to do, let the Lord do it.

Deuteronomy 32:35: "To me belongeth vengeance, and recompence; their foot shall slide in due time: for the day of their calamity is at hand, and the things that shall come upon them make haste." Let God do the fixing. It's easy to want to avenge yourself, but leave that in the Lord's hand. Our job is to concentrate on His work, His ministry, and not let guile or evil or bitterness well up in our hearts.

Rewards

When David heard of Nabal's death, he "sent and communed with Abigail" (v. 39). Well, you can imagine how that happened. The letters began to go back and forth between David and Abigail. They were slow at first, and then they began to come often with only a day or two between. Abigail soon found herself anxiously waiting, watching the horizon for a sign of a runner coming with another letter. It was strange she should feel such anticipation just waiting for a letter. It was stranger still how those letters warmed and moved her heart.

And then one day as she watched out the window, over the hill came a complete entourage. Was it trouble? Abigail caught her breath and searched her mind for answers. The entourage was soldiers, all right, but they didn't appear charging for war. It looked official. But she could think of no reason government consuls would come. Nabal had left his business in order. The taxes were paid. Surely no one was coming to take over the property. Then as the caravan came closer, Abigail recognized some of the soldiers. Why, she had seen those men when she had met David in the wilderness. They must be David's men. Questions raced through Abigail's mind. Had they come for peace? Had they come for trouble?

Once more, Abigail kept her self-control in balance and went out to meet them. David's messengers were faithful and came straight to the point. "David sent us unto thee, to take thee to him to wife" (v. 40). Whew! What a shock! What a proposal! Now it's her turn to faint! Can she believe her ears? What will she do? How will Abigail respond? She could say, "Well, I've been wondering when somebody was going to recognize my beauty." Or she could have kicked up her heels and said, "I'm going to be Queen! I'm going to be Queen!" She could have been haughty and filled with pride and made the servants practice bowing down to her. But what was her response? "She arose, and bowed herself on her face to the earth, and said, Behold, let thine handmaid be a servant to wash the feet of the servants of my lord." Not just to wash his feet, but to wash his servants' feet. Abigail was always ready to serve. There was no pride in her attitude, only humility and gratitude for what the Lord had done for her. What beauty, what humility, what composure. It's no wonder that David fell in love with this gracious lady. I Peter 5:5-6: "Likewise, ye younger, submit yourselves unto the elder. Yea, all of you be subject one to another, and be clothed with humility: for God resisteth the proud, and giveth grace to the humble. Humble yourselves therefore under the mighty hand of God, that he may exalt you in due time." That's just what Abigail did. She humbled herself, and God lifted her up at His time and in His way.

Abigail was ready to go. "She hasted." There's that phrase again. She didn't even stop to talk to her handmaids about what kind of wedding she should have or what dress she would wear. Verse 42: "And Abigail hasted, and arose, and rode upon an ass, with five damsels of hers that went after her; and she went after the messengers of David, and became his wife."

All of the blessings and privileges of the coming king now belonged to Abigail. Let me tell you, though, those blessings were awhile in coming, because that was no bridal suite Abigail had out there in the wilderness. She and David were doing nothing but camping out for awhile with six hundred rough soldiers at hand. That was not exactly a honeymoon cottage, but Abigail was willing to take those hard times in order to share the life and the blessings of David. And that's what marriage is all about. You know, when you get married everything will not be a bed of roses. There will be hard times and there will be good times, but the joy is in being in God's service and doing His will together. Abigail might have been "Miss Abigail" to the servants, she might have been "Lady Abigail" to the people of Judah, but to David, she was his own "Dear Abby." Oh, those tender words were music to her ears. And you will be "dear" and "precious" to the husband that God gives you if you're faithful and true to Him.

Chapter 3

II Kings 4: The Shunammite

There was a program on television called "Who's Who." There is an organization called "Who's Who in American Colleges and Universities." There is a book entitled *Personalities of the South.* There are many ways the world recognizes leaders, but God has a special "Who's Who."

If you will look in Hebrews 11, you will find a thriller. People the world ordinarily recognizes are small compared to God's heroes. Begin with verse 36: "And others had trial of cruel mockings and scourgings, yea, moreover of bonds and imprisonments: They were stoned, they were sawn asunder, were tempted, were slain with the sword: they wandered about in sheepskins and goatskins; being destitute, afflicted, tormented; (Of whom the world was not worthy)." The world would have counted the people listed here as scum and offscouring, but God put their names in the bright lights of heaven and recorded them in history in His

"Who's Who." The lady we are studying now is referred to in this list. She is not mentioned by name, but she is bound to be one of those acknowledged in verse 35: "Women received their dead raised to life again." Turn, please, to II Kings 4:8. "And it fell on a day, that Elisha passed to Shunem, where was a great woman; and she constrained him to eat bread. And so it was, that as oft as he passed by, he turned in thither to eat bread."

Oh, there is an on-the-scene reporter. He has stopped this woman on the street. Let's listen to the interview.

"Madam," the reporter begins, "you are a Shunammite lady. We noticed that you are recorded in the Word of God as a 'great woman.' To what do you attribute this great success? Why does God call you a great woman?"

The Shunammite woman stands there rather hesitantly, looking a little embarrassed, and says, "You know, I haven't the faintest idea why God would put such an adjective by my name. I surely don't consider myself great."

"Would it be because of your heritage or that you come from a great city?"

"Well, no, I'm sure it couldn't be that. Shunem is just a little town, a sort of out-of-the-way place about twenty miles from the Sea of Galilee. We don't have any especially historic monuments or attractions. My people are ordinary, hard-working people. No, I don't think that could be the reason."

"Well, maybe it is because you are wealthy." Certainly the world responds to people who have big bank accounts, or property, or valuable antiques, or stocks and bonds. The world bows to wealth and money. If you have a lot of money, you are "Mr. So and So" when you walk into the bank. If you don't have much money, you can stand and wait in line and get lost in the crowd. You're just a nobody. This world bows to wealth. "Maybe your wealth is why God called you a great woman, Madam."

"Oh, no," she said. "You know, God has been wonderfully good to us, but we certainly aren't wealthy." And she wasn't. When a woman can name the furniture in a room in her house on four fingers—a bed, a table, a stool, and a candlestick—you can't call her wealthy. She had her needs supplied, but she surely wasn't rich. No, it couldn't be the wealth of this world that gave her such a title.

"Maybe it's because you are rather large physically."

"Well, no, you can plainly see that's not the reason. Oh, the Lord blesses us, and we eat well, but I work most of it off. No, I stay trim and healthy as I should."

Why did God call her great? As we study the Word, I think we will see why God called her great. The answer begins in that same verse we read. "She constrained him to eat bread. And so it was, that as oft as he passed by, he turned in thither to eat bread."

Hospitality

Hospitality is the first quality that made her great in God's sight. I Timothy 3:2 says: Be "given to hospitality." Many passages of Scripture refer to having your home open to God's people. It is necessary in a Christian home that people know they have a welcome with you. This was evident in Elisha's situation here. He may have gone through other towns thirsty and hungry with nobody inviting him in. At nightfall he may have had to spend the night in a cave or under the trees or wherever he could find shelter. But when he came to Shunem, he always had a place to stay. This lady was given to hospitality. She was looking out for God's servant. He didn't have to be concerned about whether he would go to bed without supper that night. He didn't have to be concerned about whether he could find a place out of the rain. He found a welcome at the Shunammite woman's home.

Compassion

She was also a very compassionate woman. "And so it was, that as oft as he passed by, he turned in thither to eat bread." She knew Elisha had needs. Proverbs 31:20: "She stretcheth out her hand to the poor; yea, she reacheth forth her hands to the needy." No doubt this woman was very busy, yet she took time to realize that other people had problems and needs. When Elisha came hot, dusty, lonely, tired, having been mocked and rejected in other places, her heart went out to God's servant, and she welcomed him into her home. Oh, the joy of having a compassionate heart and being able to see other people's needs. We get wrapped up in our own problems, but this Shunammite woman had learned how to be compassionate. She had learned how to bear another's burdens. She couldn't carry the heavy spiritual load that Elisha carried, but she could help him by being hospitable.

"She reacheth forth her hands to the needy"

(Prov. 31:20). "Withhold not good from them to
whom it is due, when it is in the power of thine hand
to do it" (Prov. 3:27). If there is a way to help and it is
in our power to do it, as Christians we ought to have
compassionate hearts and step forward as the
Shunammite woman did. Unconcern is the reason
the welfare program has come in like a flood. Old
folks' homes (state and private) are full because
people are not bearing their own responsibilities. I
realize that sometimes people are ill physically, so
that they cannot be cared for at home. They need a
hospital or professional care. I am not saying that
everyone who is in such a home or institution is
there because nobody loves him or her. Sometimes
families have to place a loved one there for the
person's benefit, but you know yourself, old folks'
homes these days are filled with elderly people who
have been "dumped," because their children have
disregarded them. They would rather pay money
than have them in their way, interfering with their
schedules. We have known old people in old folks'
homes whose children never came to see them.
Some came only once a year. That is sad. That is not
right, and as Christian people we especially should
be concerned. If people who were genuinely in need
were cared for by their own people, their own
neighbors, or the church folks, there wouldn't be a
need for so many government welfare programs.
Government has taken the responsibility away, and
now the whole situation is nearly out of hand.

Proverbs 31:20: "She stretcheth out her hand to
the poor; yea, she reacheth forth her hands to the
needy." Of course, this includes not only meeting
physical needs but also having a compassionate

heart as a soulwinner. That type of person has the heart to be able to see past the outward look of people and see the heart underneath that needs the Lord Jesus Christ as Saviour. She has the heart to take the time to witness and to lead someone to the Lord. A compassionate heart in prayer and in witnessing is all-important. I believe the Shunammite's hospitality and compassion are the first two reasons this woman is called "great" in the Word of God.

Spiritual Perception

The next thing for which the Shunammite woman is great is her spiritual perception. Notice verse 9: "And she said unto her husband, Behold now, I perceive that this is an holy man of God, which passeth by us continually." She had watched Elisha go through town; a few days later, she would see him on his return journey. She had seen his consistent testimony, and it had touched her heart. She had spiritual perception, and she finally said to her husband, "I perceive that this man is an holy man of God." That, my dears, is remarkable, because nobody else in the world had perceived it. King Jehoram of Israel hadn't perceived it. He was a wicked and evil man; he hated the mention of Elisha's name. He surely didn't perceive that Elisha was a holy man.

The king of Judah, Jehoshaphat, didn't perceive that Elisha was a holy man either. The only time he wanted Elisha around was when he wanted Elisha to get him out of trouble. Jehoshaphat was a compromiser. He would forge ahead and do what he wanted to do, and then he wanted Elisha to come to his rescue. Elisha was welcome only at

Jehoshaphat's convenience, so he didn't recognize Elisha's position as a man of God.

The people of the territory didn't recognize it. Just a few days before, Elisha had passed through Bethel, and the children had mocked him, "Go up, thou bald head! Go up, thou bald head." Now where do you think those children got that kind of attitude toward God's prophet? They had heard Mom and Dad and other adults low-rating and saying what scum Elisha was, and the adults' attitudes came out in the children. Oh, how true that is. Parents need to be careful what they say about other people and what their attitude is at home toward the pastor, teachers, and other Christians. You think you will keep your words behind closed doors, but they will come out; your true attitudes will come out through your children. They were making fun of Elisha. They mocked him, they hated him, they rejected his preaching and his miracles. They surely did not recognize him as a man of God.

Even God's people did not recognize Elisha as a man of God. When Elijah went up in the clouds and Elisha came back through the Jordan, the sons of the prophets did not believe Elisha's words. They insisted on an expedition to search for Elijah's body. When Elisha declared that there was no need to go, they wouldn't believe his word. They had no confidence in Elisha. So even the prophets, God's people, didn't perceive, as the lady said, that he was a "holy man of God."

What a remarkable woman! She had a spiritual perception that had to come from seeking the Lord, from having a heart in tune with the Lord with no sin between. You cannot have this kind of perception with any known sin or self-will between yourself and the Lord. The Lord will not reveal things to one who rejects His truth or does not obey His Word. God in a wonderful way gave her a heart, an ear, and an eye for God's servant and God's work. She was a remarkable woman and was listed as "great" because of her spiritual perception.

Self-Sacrifice

Another quality was her self-sacrifice. "And she said unto her husband, Behold now, I perceive that this is an holy man of God, which passeth by us continually. Let us make a little chamber, I pray thee, on the wall; and let us set for him there a bed, and a table, and a stool, and a candlestick: and it shall be, when he cometh to us, that he shall turn in thither."

The Shunammite woman not only recognized that Elisha was God's man, but she wanted to do something to help him in God's work. She was not a preacher; she could not get out and carry the message to other cities; she could not work the miracles; but she knew she could uphold God's man in prayer. She knew she could fix him some chicken and biscuits when he came to town. She wanted to support him and do anything possible to help in God's work. She backed up her religious words with action. Talk is cheap. It is easy to talk "spiritual," but it is another story to back up the holy, pious talk with actual words and deeds. This project cost her money. The money she paid for building materials and extra furniture could have been spent on new clothes or a new chariot, but this Shunammite sacrificed her own desires in order to support God's servant. She put her money into the work of the Lord.

She also gave her own energy and strength. She took in this guest never knowing when he was coming. That was an inconvenience. It meant extra food, extra cleaning, and extra preparation. She had to stay ready all the time because she never knew when Elisha would come. It would have been much easier for her just to speak to Elisha and let him pass by, but every time Elisha came, she hastened to attend to his needs. It was work. It took time to cook supper, clean the room, make the bed, wash the linen. Yet she was willing to take time away from the other things that were pressing her. She cared not for herself; she cared only what she could do for the Lord and for His servant. Say, she surely would have been out of place today. The proponents of ERA would have hated this gal, wouldn't they? They would have downed her from here to Washington. She would not have been at home in the trend and philosophy of this world. What is that advertisement? "Oh, I do many things for my family, but I take this tonic for myself." "For myself," would you believe? She devours the stuff so she can have energy to do her own business and look out for "Number One." That ad takes the cake, but the one that tops them all is the advertisement for a certain shampoo. I cringe and get ashamed for that woman. With her seductive look she says, "I know it's more expensive, but then *I'm worth it!*" Can you imagine the pride of a woman who feels that way? That is the inner attitude of many people these days, because the public schools' philosophy has put so much emphasis on humanism. Public schools have trained children through child-centered education and the philosophy of self-expression until pride is accepted. Oh, pardon me—the progressive educators wouldn't call it pride; they call it having a good "self-image." Say, if you bring up a girl with that type of teaching of self-image and a little bit of Spock's philosophy, when she gets grown you will have a self-centered monster! She will be a woman (not a lady) who looks out for "Number One," who thinks she is a glamor doll, and that every man ought to swoon when she passes by. She will be so vain she will imagine that every man turns his head and gapes after her. He may turn and gape all right—not because of her charm, but because she is a public spectacle! This Shunammite woman surely would not have been at home in our day, and as a Christian woman you are going to be out of place too. If you really walk close to the Lord, govern your life according to the principles of the Word of God, dress modestly, and walk discreetly and in the fear of the Lord, you are going to be a misfit. You are going to be out of place in this present world. People are going to say, "What a square she is!" But that's all right. You're looking for God's approval, not man's.

Openness

Before we go on, please notice the way this woman approached her husband about the room for Elisha. Do you notice that there seemed to be no preparation for it? All of a sudden she says to her husband, "Behold now, I perceive that this is an holy man of God. Let's make him a little chamber." I think she had a good, open relationship with her husband. Through years of marriage, she had not learned to connive behind her husband's back or to see what she could get out of her husband by getting his promises without his realizing the trap had been laid. It is important in marriage that there are no secrets between husband and wife. What he does and thinks is open to you; what you do and think is open to him.

There is such a thing as a woman getting her way by conniving and trickery. For instance, suppose lovely spring weather has come and the wife wants a new spring suit. So she goes shopping and finds her dream outfit. It is darling—just what she has always wanted. It is the perfect color and a perfect fit. It costs a little more than she has ever paid for clothes before; it is really beyond their budget; but she surely would like to have it. So she begins to plot. The apple pie comes out to top off his favorite supper; the button that has been off his shirt is suddenly sewn on; not a word is said about his clothes being left on the chair. The little things that he would appreciate just happen to get done. She knows just how to manage. And at just the right time she says, "About that suit . . ." Well, she has been so good to him; she has been on such good behavior for so many days that he could not afford to tell her, "No." So she gets the suit. Now I believe if a wife gets the outfit that way, it will smite her conscience every time she puts it on. That pretty outfit that looked so fashionable modeled on a mannequin in the store will never be a pleasure when she gets it home. The best things, obtained under false pretenses, will never be a joy or blessing.

There are many ways women need to watch themselves in being aboveboard with their husbands, not conniving, not using trickery or bribery. Wives can use even their own bodies, physical love, to bribe their husbands. The unspoken threat is, "If you don't give me what I want or let me have my way, I will withhold my love; I will withhold myself from you." How pitiful to stoop to such. Husbands and wives are to be one flesh. One is not to reserve herself for selfish reasons or purposes. Love is to be genuine, deep, real, and unselfish. Be careful not to use trickery, false motives, or false pretenses. Be so open with your husband that you can talk plainly about everything. This promises perfect trust.

Reasonableness

Did you notice her husband's response? It is amazing! Here was a woman wanting to remodel the house, and the man didn't even argue. I think there was a very good reason. I think she had proved herself to be a reasonable woman. The further you go into the chapter, the more you realize that through the years she had been careful and wise. Her husband watched her through the years and had come to respect her judgment and the requests that she made because they were not selfish. When she wanted something, it was for a right reason and a good purpose. It was for the good of the family and the welfare of the home. He had learned to respect her judgment so that when she came up with a need or request, he was willing to give it full consideration. I think her husband had a deep respect for his wife, which is so important to a successful marriage.

Well, they built the addition on to the house. It

was a very plain room, but it surely was better than what Elisha usually had to sleep in. It had a bed, a table, a chair, and a candlestick—the necessities. That's the way they had learned to live—not fancy, not always wanting something else.

Verse 11: "It fell on a day, that he came thither, and he turned into the chamber, and lay there." I imagine Elisha was hot, dusty, and tired. When he came around the bend that day and saw the extra room on the house, he was surprised. He thought, "Well, I didn't know they were planning to build on to their house. It surely does look nice. I'm sure they are glad to have more room." Elisha never dreamed it was for him. A man of Elisha's caliber never would have expected somebody to have done something extra for him. He knew he would have supper with them though, as she always fixed for him when he came, so when he turned out of the dusty road and knocked on her door, she greeted him in the same joyous manner. "Today I have a surprise for you, Elisha. Come and see." And she showed him the room. It was just about more than Elisha could take in. At last, he went in and shut the door. I'm sure he lay down on the bed, put his hands behind his head, lay there looking at the ceiling, and marveled at the whole situation. It was just too good to believe that he had a place to stay and these folks had shown their love to him in such a wonderful way.

Now there's the key to Elisha's greatness—he had a thankful heart. You know there are many people who would have taken such kindness for granted. They would have said, "Well, I come here a lot of times; they ought to be expecting me. It's only right. I am God's man, and they ought to fix supper for me." There are ingrates in this world who feel just that way. They expect favors, and they take for granted the things people do for them. Dr. Bob Jones, Sr. used to say, "When gratitude dies on the altar of a man's heart, that man is well nigh hopeless."

Contentment

There Elisha lay, resting from the heat and the weary walk, when all of a sudden he must have sat straight up on the bed and fairly hollered at his servant. Half-startled, Gehazi came running. Elisha said, "Call this Shunammite." Now this was remarkable. "And he said unto him, Say now unto her, Behold, thou hast been careful for us with all this care; what is to be done for thee?"

Elisha wanted to reward her kindness. He had no money. How did he think he would reward the woman? He had no way to pay her. But he said, "Look, you've been so good to me. This is just wonderful. I could never repay you, but is there anything I could do for you?"

"Well," she thought, "I appreciate it, but you know we put this room on because we just wanted to do something for you."

"Yes, I know that, but let me do something in return."

"Well, I appreciate it, but I just can't think of anything I need."

"Could I speak to the king for you or to the captain of the host?"

Now see her answer. "I dwell among mine own people." I tell you, here is a phenomenon. Here is a woman, one of the feminine gender, a female of the species, who had no complaints, no gripes, no wants, no wishes. She was perfectly satisfied with what God had given her in life. Now, that was remarkable. She had learned how to be content in God's service with whatever He had supplied. What a testimony! I suppose if we had walked into her house we probably could have thought of a half dozen things she could have used. As earthly as we are, we, no doubt, could have helped her list many things for which to ask, but in her heart, she had no wants. She was perfectly satisfied. Oh, what a wonderful testimony to God's grace for a Christian woman to be satisfied in the Lord Jesus Christ. What a joy to find a Christian homemaker who is not seeking the things of this world. What does Luke 12:15 say? "Beware of covetousness: for a man's life consisteth not in the abundance of the things which he possesseth." That is opposite from the world's philosophy today. The world thinks "things" will satisfy.

Recently, I was in town in a gift shop. The store would just take your breath away with all the lovely pieces of sparkling crystal and gleaming silver. It reminded me of what children must feel in a gigantic toy store. Their eyes get big and they are unable to take in all the wonders. I said to the clerk, "What do you do when you work here around these beautiful things all day?" She said, "Well, you buy until you have a house full." I marveled at people having so much to buy. She said even older women who have silver and china from early years of marriage are laying that aside and buying more new patterns and pieces because the new things are so beautiful. The things of the world have luster and

appeal and sparkle, but as a Christian wife you have
to decide what is right for you and what you need
and just pass the other by. Those things are for folks
who have more means and whose sights are just in
this world. We need to be satisfied with what God
has given us instead of wanting every new thing we
see. A Christian just can't live that way. Just
because everybody else has all that fancy stuff
doesn't necessarily mean we need it. This world has
gone mad on "things." It's hard to believe how many
"things" there are for people to have if their hearts
are set on this world's treasures, but we Christians
need "godliness with contentment." I Timothy 6:6
says, "But godliness with contentment is great
gain." Verse 8: "And having food and raiment let us
be therewith content." Our mind does not need to
be on the treasure and gain of this world. Our
money, our time, our thoughts, our energy, our
"treasure" need to be invested in the Lord's work.
"For where your treasure is, there will your heart be
also" (Matt. 6:21). Be satisfied with what God has
given you. If he gives you more today than yesterday
say, "Thank you, Lord," and use it for His glory. But
don't have your heart set on more things of this
world. Psalm 62:10: "If riches increase, set not your
heart upon them." Young people think "things" will
meet every need. A teenager thinks if he only had a
car, he would be happy. A girl thinks if she only had
a new formal for the party, she would be happy. A
girl thinks, "If I only had a job and a fine apartment,
I'd be happy." But the minute that desire is fulfilled it
fades into insignificance, and they are wanting
something else.

If you build your life on things, you are on sinking sand, and you will never be happy, but if you "seek first the kingdom of God and His righteousness," God promises that all "these things" will be added. You will have your needs supplied. Philippians 4:19 says, "My God shall supply all your need according to his riches in glory by Christ Jesus." He has all the riches in the world. He will supply them when we need them, if we learn to have a heart content and satisfied in Him. So, as Paul, in whatever state or condition she was, the Shunammite woman had learned to be content.

But Elisha lay there and thought, "She's satisfied and that's great, but I am going to do something for that woman somehow." And he kept urging his servant, "Gehazi, what does she need? There has to be something that would please the woman so that we can show her our gratitude." Most of us would have been relieved. We would have shrugged, "Well, I tried," but Elisha was determined to find a way to show his appreciation.

At last Gehazi suggested, "Verily she hath no child, and her husband is old." Elisha jumped. "That's it, Gehazi! You've hit it; that's it!" His heart was thrilled because God had revealed the very desire of her heart.

Surrender

I'm sure as a young woman the Shunammite had spent hours in prayer asking God for a baby. Every woman wants to be a mother. It is a desire that God has put down deep inside the heart. She no doubt spent many hours in prayer and shed many tears that God would give them children and that their home would be blessed with the chatter and clatter of little folks. But the years passed, and no baby came. Her husband evidently was quite a bit older than she, and I imagine after time passed and they both began to get up in years, she just laid that request aside and was satisfied with the Lord's will in the matter. She probably said to herself, "Well, the years have piled up. God has not granted my petition, but I'm not going to stay in a stew about it for the rest of my life. God knows best." Now God always answers. It may be "Yes," or "No," or "Wait awhile," but when some people don't get a "Yes" answer they get bitter at God or anyone else on whom they can vent their wrath. Not so with this Shunammite. She was willing to say to God, "All right, God, Thy decision is final. I'll table the matter." I'm sure that as far as she was concerned the matter was settled with the Lord. But God has a wonderful way of seeing down into the depths of the heart when we have yielded everything to Him. Psalm 37:4: "Delight thyself also in the Lord; and he shall give thee the desires of thine heart." God will supply all our needs, but when we are really yielded to Him, He has a wonderful way of satisfying the deep desires of our heart as well. Often, at the least expected time, God brings blessings down. That is one of the joys of being one hundred percent yielded and dedicated to the Lord. At the most unexpected time God rains showers of blessings, and you stand in awe at how wonderful God is. Let's see how it happened to the Shunammite woman.

II Kings 4:16: Elisha called her in, "And he said, About this season, according to the time of life, thou shalt embrace a son." That was quite an announcement, wasn't it? How would you like to receive a baby announcement that way? Here she was up in years; her husband was past the reproductive years; humanly speaking this was impossible. But don't forget, God is the God of the impossible. Luke 1:37: "For with God nothing shall be impossible." Genesis 18:14 asks, "Is any thing too hard for the Lord?" Why, no! And at the least expected time, here was the announcement: "About this time . . . thou shalt embrace a son." It's a wonder she didn't faint! By her answer, I think her face must have turned pale, her knees went limp, her arms got weak, no smile broke across her face; it was a total shock. Now this Shunammite woman had faith. She believed Elisha was a man of God, so when he spoke, she immediately took his words for fact. She didn't doubt, but it was such a big promise that she said, "Nay, my lord, thou man of God, do not lie unto thine handmaid."

Discretion

You know, there are some things in life that are not to be joked about. I think every Christian woman with a compassionate heart needs to ask God for help to understand people. It is important to know when to laugh with someone, to know when to cry with someone, to know when to joke and tease, and when to be totally serious. The book of Ecclesiastes has a great deal to say about that: "A time to weep, and a time to laugh; a time to mourn, and a time to dance." There is a proper time for everything. Christians need to be sensitive to the Spirit of God, so that we can respond to people's needs in the right way. To her, this was no joking matter, and so it is to many people with problems in their lives.

Sometimes children come to adults with problems only to have their problems taken lightly. I remember a particular time when I was busy in the auditorium and a young high school boy came to me. "Mrs. Hobbs," he spoke softly, "I . . . I want to talk to you."

"Sure," I said, "what is it?"

He was stammering and stalling, but it was one of those very busy times and I said, "Go ahead, I'm listening." Then I looked at his face and knew immediately that this problem needed more attention than a little "You keep talking while I keep working" chat. We went to the privacy of the office and sat down. "Now," I said, "what's the problem? Let's talk." You know there are times when all your "busy" isn't worth a nickel. There are times when you can just let your "business" jump overboard, because someone's need is more important.

"Well, I . . . I," he stammered.

"Go on, spill it, Johnny. Unload."

The look of distress and worry deepened in his eyes. "Well, I . . . there's this girl."

"Yes?"

"I won her to the Lord last week."

"Well, that's wonderful!"

"Yes, but she called me up last night," he choked, "and she wants to marry me!"

Then I nearly choked! This was ridiculous! My first impulse was to lean back and laugh, but I dared not! Here was a boy of fifteen with a problem as big as a mountain on his shoulders. It had made him nearly sick. He certainly didn't want to marry the girl, but he didn't want to shake her as a new Christian and make her think he wasn't concerned either. This was no time to make light, and we talked the whole thing out as seriously as if he had been a mature young man facing matrimony.

As a parenthesis, let me say that this story is an example of how the devil works. Here was a boy who had dedicated his life to the Lord and was serious about being a witness. He had witnessed and won a girl to the Lord, and the devil took that same very worthy and honorable deed and made it treachery in his life. Now listen, you pray for your kids—not only your own children but also for the young people in your church and in your neighborhood. They need your prayers desperately. The devil has more tricks and traps to lay before them than you and I can imagine. Just when you think they're going to move out for the Lord and really take their stand, the devil will find something to put across their path to trip them and send them smashing on their faces. You had better pray for them morning, noon, and night, and all hours in between. The devil is not going to let them come through for the Lord without a fight. First of all, he will work to keep them from getting saved, and after that, you needn't think he will quit. He will give them a battle for the rest of their lives.

True, there are times when laughing and teasing are in order, but there are also times which require serious thought and response. When God's prophet announced the birth of a son, the Shunammite said, "Oh, Elisha, don't joke with me, don't tease me about this." You see, he had gone to

the very core of her heart. He had touched that
unspoken request which she had not been able to
share with anyone, that deep heart's desire that was
between only her and the Lord. And she said,
"Please don't joke with me about this, Elisha."

"I'm not joking," he said quickly, for he wouldn't
have offended her. "This is God's promise: 'Thou
shalt embrace a son.'"

Some nine months or so later, a kicking, cooing,
darling baby boy was rocking in a handmade cradle
in the Shunammite's home. It was wonderful how
God had worked miraculously to enable her to bring
a child into the world. What a change came to that
house. She and her husband had begun to get old
together, set in their ways, and were used to their
routines when this little live wire came along and
upset the schedule completely. What a joyful home
it must have been. What a thrill it must have been
when she saw the baby begin first creeping, and
then crawling, and then toddling. She taught him
how to talk. She taught him to sing. She taught him
to pray. She taught him early to speak God's name
reverently. She taught him all the lessons that
Christians teach their little ones. But, as boys do, he
began to grow up. He got to be a good-sized tyke
when "it fell on a day, that he went out to his father
to the reapers. And he said unto his father, My head,
my head." Suddenly he had a splitting headache.
Something snapped. Whether or not there had
been any symptoms or warning earlier, we don't
know; but suddenly the child was in severe pain. He
ran to his father crying, "My head, my head!"

And the father said to a lad, "Carry him to his

mother." Now isn't that just like a man. The boy had been out with him all day, running and playing and beginning to learn to work alongside his dad. The proud father talked and laughed with him and taught him many lessons, but the minute something went wrong the immediate response was, "Take him to his mother." Well, that's all right. That's what mothers are for. That is what your lap was made for. God gave you a soft one just right for cuddling and holding your little lambs. And He gave you a tender heart to be able to understand the bruises and the bumps and the heartaches.

So the lad carried the boy to his mother, and she took him and held him in her lap till noon. Oh, those hours must have been endless agony as she gently moved forward and back in the chair. She held the boy close to her breast. She felt his fever rise. There was no doctor for whom to send. There was nothing she could offer beyond the cool, damp cloth for his head and the security of a mother's love. The situation had to rest in God's hands. All she could do was sit and hold him close and pray. I imagine tears rolled down her face in spite of her efforts to fight them back. She quickly wiped them from her cheeks to keep them from falling on the boy. She dared not let the child know that his mother was upset. She had to be strong before him, and she comforted and she sang. She talked reassuringly and told him more of God and His love. But about noontime, his breathing stopped, and he lay still and lifeless in her arms.

Now what would you have done if that had been your child? The question is worth consideration. Some mothers would have fallen apart and gone

into hysteria. Some would have gone screaming and
crying for somebody to come help. But this woman
had a sense of composure and a strength of
character even in the face of heartache. Nothing but
the grace of God could have given her this spirit of
composure. This peace is the fruit of total
surrender. She had confidence, as dark as the hour
seemed, that there was nothing between her and
the Lord. She was walking in fellowship with the
Lord, and whatever happened was His will. She had
trusted Him completely, and the grace of God gave
her a quiet spirit.

She gently laid the child on the bed of the man of
God, shut the door, and softly went out. No panic,
no frenzy. In this moment of sorrow and tension,
she sent to her husband for a donkey. She said,
"Send me, I pray thee, one of the young men, and
one of the asses, that I may run to the man of God
and come again."

And he said, "Wherefore wilt thou go to him to
day? It is neither new moon, nor sabbath." Well,
isn't that just like a man? She makes a simple
request, and he says, "What do you want to do that
for? It's not the Sabbath." It was like a present-day
husband's comments: "What do you need the car
for today?" Husbands always want to know where,
why, when. It's amazing. A man can work all day
away from home and come in much later than
expected. He can take a whole day to go golfing or
fishing. He can be gone a week or two on business
or to attend a conference. He can be gone for a
dozen reasons, but if you go out of the house for
fifteen minutes, he asks, "Where are you going?"
You can start out the door just to carry out the

trash, and you hear, "Where are you going?" You can start the car, and he calls, "How long are you going to be gone?" Even if you only have to run to the store for a loaf of bread, it's "Where are you going? How long are you going to be gone?" You take a deep breath and think, "Mister, you have been gone all day, and now I'm leaving for two minutes flat and you want to know where, why, and all about it." Yes, but don't resent it. Be glad he cares. You see, a house does not make a home; you and your husband and your children, if you have any, make a home. So don't begrudge his not wanting you to be gone even for a little while. Consider it a compliment. Hide it like a treasure in your heart when he wants to know where you are going, what you are going to do, and when you will be back—not because he doesn't trust you, but simply because home is not home if you're not there. Be grateful and humble knowing that he doesn't even want to be at home if the house is empty. Treasure and nurture such love. Handle it with care. Many women of wealth would trade their jewels and deep carpets and cut crystal for love like that. Social prestige and bank accounts cannot substitute for the deep, abiding love of a Christian husband. Places and things cannot compare with your husband's person and presence. Build the kind of companionship that makes each passing year richer and sweeter—not more cold or bitter. "Every wise woman buildeth her house" (Prov. 14:1).

"Wherefore will you go?" She answered, "Don't worry. Everything is okay." She didn't cry out about the tragedy. She didn't even tell him the boy was dead. She said only, "It shall be well."

With her heart pounding and hands trembling, she saddled the ass and commanded the servant, "Drive, and go forward; slack not thy riding for me, except I bid thee." She knew the servant would be worried about her welfare, but her comfort was of no consequence at a time like this.

So she went to the man of God at Mount Carmel. At his master's word, Gehazi ran out to meet her. "Is it well with thee? Is it well with thy husband? Is it well with the child?" And she answered, "It is well." Her husband was away working in the field; her only son was dead, and she said, "All is well." Such confidence can only be in the Lord God of heaven. "All is well." With such deep need and concern of heart, she kept her composure and proved God's grace to be sufficient. Such character in the face of heartache! What a touching testimony! I tip my hat in honor as I see her pass by. I bow my head in humility in the presence of fearless, dauntless, shameless faith. Let the dry sands of dearth and destitution sift down to the barest floor. Let the winds of sorrow blow. Let the breakers of tragedy beat and roll. This faith stands—keeps on standing—and even moves forward against the wave of the storm. Oh, to walk with saints like this who stood yielded to God when the odds were against them—the Shunammite, Esther, Daniel, Paul, Martin Luther. Stand, if you will, by the side of Rachel Elliott whose missionary husband was killed by the very Indians he sought to evangelize. Stand with her as faith quenches resentment and she whispers, "All is well," and goes in person to carry the gospel to that heathen tribe. Stand, if you dare, by Charles T. Studd as he signs away all his father's vast fortune, facing the rebuke and disdain of family and friends, counting all but loss to go to foreign soil and claim his beloved China for Christ Jesus. In the face of loneliness and being forsaken, he says, "All is well." Stand with those who had the faith and character and surrender to do God's will even in the face of heartache. Then you, too, by faith, may breathe, "All is well," and see God's hand at work when no one else understands.

Does Jesus Care?

Does Jesus care when my heart is pained
Too deeply for mirth or song;
As the burdens press, and the cares distress,
And the way grows weary and long?

Does Jesus care when my way is dark
With a nameless dread and fear?
As the daylight fades into deep night shades,
Does he care enough to be near?

Does Jesus care when I've tried and failed
To resist some temptation strong;
When for my deep grief I find no relief,
Though my tears flow all the night long?

Does Jesus care when I've said "goodbye"
To the dearest on earth to me,
And my sad heart aches till it nearly breaks,
Is it aught to Him? Does He see?

Oh yes, He cares; I know He cares,
His heart is touched with my grief;
When the days are weary, the long nights dreary,
I know my Saviour cares.

—Frank E. Graeff

Notice now, that the woman quickly passed by

Gehazi and went directly to Elisha. The secret of
getting help is taking your need to the right person.
If advice is needed, get it from a godly person who
will direct you to the Word of God for the answer
rather than to the thinking or philosophies of man.
The Shunammite knew she had to take her problem
to God's man because anyone else would be
insufficient. She fell at his feet and would not leave
him. "As the Lord liveth, and as thy soul liveth, I will
not leave thee." How much like that should we be
with the Lord. Our prayer needs to be directly to the
Lord God in heaven, and we should be persistent
and earnest before Him. Yet sometimes we make
our requests everywhere else first. We run to the
banker; we run to the neighbors; we run to
Grandma; we run to the preacher; and then, as if as
a last resort, we come to God. These other sources
may well be concerned, but we had better learn to
run first to the Lord Jesus Christ. "Let us therefore
come boldly unto the throne of grace, that we may
obtain mercy, and find grace to help in time of need"
(Heb. 4:16).

    "When Elisha was come into the house, behold,
the child was dead, and laid upon his bed. He went in
therefore, and shut the door upon them twain, and
prayed unto the Lord." You know the rest of the
story: how he lay upon the child, face against face,
hands against hands, body against body. As Elisha
breathed, the child began to wax warm. Elisha then
prayed and stretched himself seven times upon the
child, and the child sneezed. I imagine that sneeze
was like music to Elisha's ears. Usually when a child

sneezes, his mother runs for the nearest remedy. But in this case that sneeze was music from heaven. Seven times that boy sneezed and then opened his eyes. Elisha called Gehazi, Gehazi called the Shunammite, and what a happy reunion they had. She had laid her son down a cold, stiff, lifeless little form, and now she took him up warm, sneezing, breathing, happy as a bug, and hugging his mother for dear life.

Gratitude

I tell you, that was one night she was glad to cook supper and put that child up to the table. But notice what she did first. She fell at Elisha's feet and bowed herself to the ground. The first thing she did was thank the Lord. She showed her gratitude and heartfelt thanks for what the Lord had done.

We ought to be thankful for the least thing anyone does for us, and we ought to teach our children to be thankful. It is difficult to teach children to say, "Thank you." You have to work constantly to teach them to be grateful. You have to start when they are tiny tots, when they first begin to speak, and then remind them every time. I don't know when it ever becomes automatic for a child to say, "Thank you." Just about the time you think you have instilled it in him, he will lapse into grabbiness again, and you have to take the cookie away and ask, "What do you say?" "Thank you." And then you can say, "You're welcome," and lay the cookie in his hands. It seems like an endless task, but, oh, it's so important to teach children to have grateful hearts. Of course, teaching little ones begins with our having grateful hearts ourselves. We need to daily, constantly thank the Lord for His blessings.

He is good to us. Just think of all He has done for you just today. Oh, you have problems, but think what a fix you would be in if God didn't keep them as small as they are. Have you ever gone around the bed post in the dark and stubbed your toe and afterwards thanked the Lord that it wasn't any worse? Have a thankful heart. Thank the Lord for His protection of you and your family from dangers that you don't know anything about. I ran over a snake in our garage the other day. He was dead when I found him, and I thought the Lord surely took care of that because I didn't even know he was there. I could just as well have walked up on him while he was still alive. See how the Lord does so many good things for you? Have a thankful and grateful heart like the Shunammite.

She had deep gratitude and great consolation because her need was met through Him. If you are true to the Lord and to His Word, and if the Lord tarries, your crisis also will come. Be mindful of this Shunammite whom God calls "great." Have character in the face of heartache, faith instead of fear, peace instead of panic. Remember God's promise, "My grace is sufficient for thee; for my strength is made perfect in weakness" (II Corinthians 12:9). "He giveth more grace" (James 4:6).

Sometimes you are a little blue, and you worry about things, don't you? We say, "That's just the way we women are," but shame on us. Being a woman is no excuse for worrying. Trust God. Trust God! And just as He did for this woman, at the right time and in the right way, He will surround you with His grace and handle the situation. He always is faithful in fulfilling His promise of Philippians 4:19: "My God shall supply all your need," and that doesn't include only money, that includes everything you need as His child.

Fellowship

Now there is one more thing, I think, that made this woman great. It is not listed in the chapter, but the evidence shows throughout her life. I think the key to her life of faith was her devotion to and close fellowship with the Lord. This was the reason she could face the crisis when it came. She was up-to-date with her devotions. I think if you had known this woman and lived in her town, you would have seen candlelight in the window early every morning. The secret of this woman's success as a wife, as a mother, and as a Christian was her rich time of devotion with the Lord every day. My friend, there is no substitute for your being inseparable from the Lord. You cannot expect things to be right between yourself and your husband until you are first in perfect harmony with the Lord. If you don't spend time with the Lord in His Word and in prayer every morning before the day begins, how can you expect to meet the problems of the day? How can you expect to answer your children's questions? How can you expect to help them through their difficulties if you don't have God's grace, fresh and warm, in your own heart?

In the Morning

I met God in the morning
When my day was at its best,
And the presence came like sunrise,
Like a glory in my breast.

All day long his presence lingered,
All day long He stayed with me,
And we sailed in perfect calmness
O'er a very troubled sea.

Other ships were torn and battered,
Other ships were sore distressed,
But the wind that seemed to drive them
Brought to us a peace and rest.

Then I thought of other mornings
With a keen remorse of mind,
When I, too, had left the moorings
With the presence left behind.

So I think I know the secret
Learned from many a troubled way.
You must seek God in the morning
If you want Him through the day.
                                        —Ralph Cushman

Mark 1:35 says, "And in the morning, rising up a great while before day, he went out, and departed into a solitary place, and there prayed." If time alone with the heavenly Father early in the morning was important to the only begotten Son of God, how much more needful it is to us.

Martin Luther, with his heavy schedule of preaching, writing, and contending for the faith, said, "I cannot get on without three hours of prayer every day." Another time he said, "I have so much to do today, I'll have to spend an extra hour in prayer." That philosophy is backwards compared to ours most of the time. "I have so much to do today," we say, "that I don't have much time to spend in prayer." Sometimes that's the reason our days get so fouled up. Things get tangled because we run ahead of God and do the washing and ironing, the calling and visiting, and all of our other work. There is no substitute for your getting into His Word every morning and spending time with Him in prayer. The secret to a successful Christian life is right there. Be faithful, lest the cost to you and your family be greater than you can ever imagine or afford.

Chapter 4

Proverbs 31:
The Virtuous Woman

The old trunk was relegated to the bunkhouse. It stayed there year after year. Hired men put their boots and other trappings on it, and no one seemed to care about the dust-covered relic. But time passed, and with the unfolding years, the old trunk has become a treasure to me.

You see, the trunk was in my mother's home when I was a little girl. When she was five years old, her mother died in childbirth. The new baby had to be taken to neighbors to be cared for, and my mother was sent down to other neighbors, the Smiths, to live. The Smiths were a fine family with a troop of rollicking boys. Mother was part of "Grandma Smith's" brood for a couple of years, and all her earthly possessions belonged in the trunk. Some time later, she was sent to Indiana to live with some cousins, and still the trunk was her home. She worked to support herself, and as soon as she was old enough, she went to Normal School. That was the equivalent of teacher's college. She began her teaching career at an early age and taught in little country schools where one teacher taught all eight grades in one room and also carried in the coal, built the fire, swept the floor, and shouldered the whole load. (Such was the dedication of teachers of that day to educating children.) Of course, the schoolteacher lived with a farm family as near the school as possible, so in a way, the trunk was still Mother's home and the place for what earthly possessions she had.

She married in 1916, and she and Dad moved to a big ranch house on a ranch they leased, and began farming. That's where the first two boys were born. And so the family grew, and the years went on. Mother and Dad worked hard and made a home larger and more lovely than in those early days, and finally the old trunk was relegated out to the bunkhouse where the hired men bunked. It never had much care or attention, but when it came time for me to go to college, the old trunk was brought out, dusted and washed, and Carolyn and the trunk left on a very lonely train to South Carolina (further away from home than either had ever been). And so, the trunk kept my stuff for several years.

After that, we married, and now the trunk is in the attic. Someday when I get time (you know, when I "retire") I am going to refurbish and reline it and move it downstairs. Its days of being laden with boots and saddle blankets are past. Its days of travel cross-country on boxcars are over. It deserves a prominent place with its family.

The old trunk has become a treasure. If it could

talk, it could tell some interesting stories and, no doubt, some secrets, too.

The trunk itself is a treasure, but in the trunk are a few other treasures. Oh, they wouldn't mean much to other people. I doubt they would bring high bids at an antique auction, but they are treasures even so.

One treasure in the trunk is what I call our heirloom quilt. You would appreciate it, I know. The quilt is well over a hundred years old. It belonged to "Aunt Mainie." Oh, her name was Mary, but we never called her that in her life. She never weighed as much as ninety pounds soaking wet. She wore her long hair slicked back absolutely straight and fastened in a tight knot above her neck. I never knew her when it wasn't silver grey. She always kept a good supply of her giant-sized, homemade sugar cookies in a big marshmallow tin in her pantry, and though children had to be on their best, quietest, most polite behavior at her house, they were always glad to go. After Uncle Henry, her husband, died, she lived alone in the farm house. Her only companions, except when relatives or church folks came by, were her Bible and her old German hymnbook. A small green plaque hung on the wall below the clockshelf. Its faded letters imprinted its powerful message indelibly on my young mind:

> *Christ is the Head of this house,*
> *The unseen guest at every meal,*
> *The silent listener to every conversation.*

If this quilt could talk, it could tell some stories, too. Every piece and block had meaning. Perhaps it could tell you that this piece came from her wedding dress, and this was a piece from Uncle Henry's shirt.

This piece would bring to mind the summer of the drought and dry dustbowl in Kansas. This one might be a reminder of the family's survival of the winter blizzard. Here's a piece from the dress she wore when the neighbor's new baby was born and she went down to care for mother and child.

Yes, the quilt is faded and fragile now, but if it could talk, it could tell of the joys and sorrows, blessings and heartaches of a few quiet but strong folks who were part of our Christian heritage.

This old heirloom quilt, with its countless pieces so carefully cut and handsewn, reminds me of a marriage put together with the right, solid, staunch ingredients. Many marriages these days are built on froth and fluff and the excitement of a wedding. Some young people get married so quickly, they really know nothing about genuine love. True marriage is built on the blizzards, the snowstorms, the sandstorms, and the deep things of life. And so, this heirloom quilt reminds me of Proverbs 31.

Virtue

Of the thirty-one verses in Proverbs 31, twenty of them, two-thirds of the chapter, are given to God's ideal woman and the right kind of marriage. In this section, the king's mother is speaking to her son. The king had many servants. All he had to do was ring a silver bell to have his desires or demands met. Perhaps his queen could have been more of a lovely ornament than a practical asset. But that certainly is not the kind of woman this chapter describes. Now if the queen was supposed to be this versatile and capable as a wife, what then should we as Christian wives be?

Let's begin our verse-by-verse study with verse ten: "Who can find a virtuous woman? for her price is far above rubies." We immediately think of a virtuous person as being morally good, chaste, and morally pure and right, not offending God or man as far as conformity to moral or divine law is concerned. In other words, virtue means worthiness, earnestness, strong character, intelligence, wisdom, discretion, and prudence before the Lord. But you ask, "Who can find a virtuous woman?" Oh, there have been some. Abraham found a virtuous wife, and Jacob found one; but in any day, because of sin, virtuous women are few. I remember twenty-five years ago when Dr. Bob Jones, Sr., used to preach about the "soiled dove of the underworld." As he preached, your heart went out in pity toward such a woman whose life was eaten away with the lusts of the flesh. Your mind pictured a woman "in the shadows, in the streets," lurking around the corner, trying to lure a young man. We feel pity for a woman in such a state, yet we know the blood of Jesus Christ can cleanse her from all sin. We know that the blood of Christ can reach deeper than the lowest "soiled dove" could go. God's grace can reach down to the lowest gutter and lift her up. If you know someone who is deep in sin, give that one the gospel, and the Lord Jesus Christ can save to the uttermost all them that come unto God by Him. Except for God's grace and protection we could be in such a condition, so we should never get haughty or have a self-righteous attitude. We ought not to condone sinful actions or a low life, but we ought to pray for those who need God's grace in this way. If twenty-five years ago such women were cropping up more and more, what do you think the situation is in this day?

"Who can find a virtuous woman?" I tell you they are fewer and farther between now than ever before. And the danger, the sad part is that such living tragedies are not just down in the slums and dark streets or in the cellar bar; they are openly in the streets, and more and more young girls are getting into trouble.

A recent article in the newspaper would have touched your heart. "'This is Florida's tale of woe,' declared Terry Cobb, state coordinator. 'In 1975, 20,485 babies were born to unwed mothers in this state.'" Think of it! In one year, in one state alone, over 20,000 babies were born to unwed mothers, and 2,053 of these mothers were from ten to fifteen years of age! Children! Children who still ought to be out swinging and playing ball! Four nine-year-old girls gave birth in Florida that year.

"Who can find a virtuous woman?" It's such a tragic story. Of course, the state educators do not call it sin. All they know to do about helping children face the consequences of their acts is to teach them sex education and birth control. My friends, that is not the answer! The answer is to keep girls pure! The answer is to keep their minds clean!

You Christian mothers, from the day your children are born, ought to start fighting to keep their minds clean. It's difficult for a child to grow up with a clean mind in this day. The daily newspaper is filled with items and pictures unfit for clean minds. Many magazines are so bad now that there are very few a Christian home can receive. Teenage magazines are filled with sex and dancing. The styles that are advertised do nothing but turn minds toward lewdness. A few years ago when our daughter was in high school, I thought it would be good to subscribe to a nice homemaking magazine to receive recipes, interior decorating ideas, and homemaking helps. So I sent off a subscription to a well-known homemaking magazine. Well, the first issue came, and I was shocked and angry. The second issue came, and I cancelled the subscription. Oh, the recipes were there all right, sandwiched between articles on sex, triangle love stories, and sensual advertisements. Even books and magazines provided for brides are misleading. You would think a magazine of wedding dresses, wedding etiquette, and other lovely bridal items would be enjoyable, but such magazines now are filled with immodest, suggestive advertisements and articles.

If you have young girls, you are going to have a fight to bring them up for the Lord. First of all, you are not going to be able to send them to public school. I would not send a girl of mine to a public school. If sending her to a public school were my only choice, I would teach her at home or let her be ignorant forever. A few weeks ago, I saw a junior high school science textbook from a public school. Many words were printed in the text to be read openly in classrooms with girls and boys together. Some of those were words I would not pronounce out loud in the company of ladies only. There are certain items a mother and daughter discuss in the privacy and modesty of their own home. There are some things that are sacred between a girl and her mother and God. But such things are now blatantly discussed in texts for public school children of both sexes. Secondly, if you allow a television at all, you are going to have to control it. Beyond the sex and violence and bad language, personal monthly supplies for women are being advertised. Do you think I would want a boy of mine seeing such subjects, having his mind stirred with questions and having his thoughts turned to physical, sensual drives? No! You had better pray daily for your children, whether they be girls or boys, to keep them virtuous, their minds clean, and their bodies pure. That's why it is important to supervise what your children read, what they see, with whom they talk, and the subjects of their conversations. God cannot use someone whose mind is continually cluttered. A child who grows up on trashy, suggestive material, even if he gets saved, is going to have to fight desperately to keep a pure mind. It is a serious matter. All some modern progressive educators know to do is to teach the consequences and say, "Take your responsibility." They don't call it sin. They don't say, "This is wrong." They don't say, "Restrain yourself." They just say, "Here are the facts." And then what do the boys and girls do? They go out and try it. They learned how in class. Do you think I'm kidding? Filmstrips show them how. You might be surprised to see some of the books in some public school libraries that are funneled into the schools by library suppliers. They are not just suggestive; some illustrate the action completely. Now do you think a child should check out that kind of library book to read? At school they learn how to do it, so they go home and practice it.

Many parents work away from home, and they

just "trust" their children. "Oh," they say, "my child will be all right. My child wouldn't do anything wrong." Many parents have disregarded their responsibility of being parents. They would rather have another dollar than protect their child's life. I say, you must, as a Christian mother, take your responsibility. People may call you old-fashioned. They may call you old fogey. That's all right. You have to supervise and chaperone your children properly. Your children may not appreciate it at the time, but they will respect you later. That doesn't mean you have to go around with horn-rimmed glasses or sit between your children and their dates in the car, but, lady, you need to be there. You may gain a reputation, but it will be one you will be thanked for later. Now you can do it. You can supervise your children in such a way that they won't dread it, and later they will appreciate it, and you may save them a heap of heartaches. I tell you, the world's best children can yield to temptation. The flesh is weak. Now strengthen your children, and by God's grace let's raise a generation so that when God asks, "Who can find a virtuous woman?" we can say, "Lord, here are a few."

"Her price is far above rubies." Yes, there are some things money can't buy. Money cannot buy the touch of a baby's little fat hand on your cheek. Money cannot buy the thrill of your baby's giggles and coos. Money cannot buy the peace and satisfaction of a home where the Lord Jesus Christ is first. Money cannot buy the love of a virtuous, faithful wife as described in this chapter. It is wonderful to find a home where true, real love is. I really think such homes are few these days. People have so many outside recreational and social activities they have little time for family. I drove past the city's recreation center a few nights ago. The place was packed with people playing, just knocking themselves out playing softball, tennis, and basketball. It looked as if the whole town was at play. Now sports are good, and exercise is necessary to keep physically fit, but when you go crazy on the subject to the extent that your family is scattered and you have no time to spend with them, you are in trouble. If you spend much time before the television, you will soon have no family fellowship. You won't know what your children are thinking, and they won't care what you are thinking. Some parents go to their bowling league or civic or social club until there is no time left for family. Say, the family is the first unit God made, and He wants that unit to be strong. He wants us to rear our young people for the Lord so that He can have a second generation coming along. Of course, you are standing for the Lord. You intend to fight for the Lord, but somehow you have to put that same kind of fight and stamina into the next generation, or who will be standing when we are gone? There are some things that money cannot buy. It is worth going without a new outfit this spring or without the second car you feel you must have or without other things in order to have time to train, to protect, and to rear your young people for the Lord.

Trustworthiness

A scriptural marriage is the kind that is built over a period of years, like the heirloom quilt. The quilt is not just an easy sheet thrown over the top for a quick cover. A quilt is put together with many little precious pieces taken from the experiences of a family and gently, tenderly, and carefully sewn together. You can't make a quilt overnight. Quilts take time and care and attention. It is tedious work; if you don't have patience, you will never make a quilt. So it is with the right kind of marriage. It is put together by tedious, tender, loving care with every little piece of life's joy and woe stitched gently and carefully and then quilted into one big, beautiful masterpiece. Of necessity, it has to be started with young love, but young love must mature into "old love," deep, abiding love. In a recipe for chicken soup, the first instruction is, "Boil one old chicken," and a note at the end of the recipe says, "Old chickens have more flavor." True, and old love is more flavorful.

"The heart of her husband doth safely trust in her" (v.11). The young love of a bride promises to love, honor, and obey. Young love says, "I'll be true; you can count on me," but "old love" has proven to a husband through years of deeds and dedication that his heart can safely trust in her. He knows it, not just by her word, but by proving her in the test. He has seen what she will do and how she will react in every situation. That makes his heart feel safe and secure because he knows her every deed and act has proven to him that she will be loyal; she will be true. No matter how tough the storms get, she will stand by him.

You can often hear the roar of a mountain stream far off in the distance through the woods as it rushes over rocks and boulders. The water is clear and cold and good, but it is noisy as it rushes over

the rocks, because it is shallow. Then you come to a
big, open, beautiful lake, and say, "My, look how still
and quiet it is." But "still water runs deep." So it is in
marriage. The first years present many new
problems and adjustments. There will be times
when you think, "Well, I surely didn't know he
would be like that," or, "I didn't know he didn't like
spare ribs!" And just when you thought you had him
all figured out, he will prove you wrong. So there are
many rocks and problems for the water to rush
over, but as the years pass, the waters begin to run
deep. No more noisy, rushing shallows but a cool,
quiet, clear surface built on the depths of
understanding, respect, trust, and intense loyalty.
The rocks of young love make the rapids show, but
as years go by and a man and wife learn to trust and
respect each other, the still waters run deep and
smooth.

You know there are some husbands, I fear, who
go off to work in the morning trusting their wives,
but they can't really "safely trust," because there
are rendezvous going on behind their backs. But in
the case of the Christian wife and the Christian
home, the husband could go off for weeks if duty
demands and never worry because he knows he has
a wife who is true to the Lord Jesus Christ. Because
of her faithfulness to the Lord and to His Word, she
will be true to her husband too, and he has no need
to worry. His heart can safely trust in her.

Loyalty

"She will do him good and not evil all the days of
her life" (v. 12). Every decision that arises she will
say, "How will it affect my husband?" She won't ask,

"How will it affect me? Will it make things easier for
me?" or "Would it be more glamorous or more fun
for me?" Her constant consideration will be, "Will it
do my husband good? Will he be better because of
what I am planning? Will he be glad if I buy this? Will
it help our home? Will it strengthen our marriage?
Will it help our relationship?" The husband of this
kind of wife can relax and be thankful because he
knows his wife will look out for his benefit.

In what ways will she do him good? She will look
out for his physical and spiritual well-being. First of
all, she will be true to him. She will be a trustworthy
wife. Perhaps it seems foolish to mention that.
When young marrieds start out, they think, "Oh,
nothing could break us up; nothing could separate
us." But it happens to couples all too often. Just
because you said the marriage vows doesn't mean
temptation is past. There comes a salesman to the
door. He is handsome and has a smooth sales pitch.
Maybe breakfast didn't go right that morning, and
your husband left in such a hurry that there was no
goodbye kiss. Then this salesman comes in calm
and collected, looking like he has the world by the
tail. Suddenly in the blur of all the commotion of the
morning somebody else looks inviting. Put up your
guard. You know God has given you your husband
to be yours to love forever. Don't be taken in by
another man's friendliness or charming ways.
Suppose another man gives you a knowing look;
that's when your knowing look has to be
suppressed. That's when you do not respond.
That's when you are sober and self-controlled.

Titus 2:4-5 says that older women should teach
younger women "to be discreet." Discretion is a

wonderful quality. Many situations that could be problems arise in life, and you need to see that you are discreet and don't put yourself in the path of temptation. For instance, let's say you are going somewhere on an airplane or bus. Here is a seat beside a man, and there is a seat beside a woman. You take the seat beside the lady. Use your discretion. Use your good sense to keep yourself out of the path of temptation. If, however, you have to sit beside a gentleman, then be sure he remains the gentleman and you remain the lady. That doesn't mean you don't speak, but there is no tone to your conversation that is out of line for a married Christian woman. Don't let yourself be put in a situation in which you ride alone in a car with another woman's husband. Hurried situations arise, and perhaps it seems the only way, but make some kind of other arrangements. You certainly have no evil intent, and God knows your heart, but "Let not then your good be evil spoken of" (Rom. 14:16). "Abstain from all appearance of evil" (I Thess. 5:22). Be discreet.

A young bride who still has her glimmer and beauty happens to see a fine, tall, handsome man, and she thinks, "Oh, isn't he handsome? I wonder if he is married." The devil can drop a thought in an instant into your mind. He can shoot a poison dart, and unless you are up-to-date in the Word of God and prayer, before you realize it, you will be entertaining that little thought. Brace yourself and say, "Lord, forgive me. Cleanse my mind." Quote the Scripture. Get your mind on the right things. Get busy doing the work at hand. Temptation is subtle, and the devil works cunningly to try to destroy a Christian's testimony.

Even couples who have been married twenty years and have children nearly grown are getting divorced. What happened? Well, they let their minds wander from the steady path. One has not been absolutely loyal and true. Dr. Bob Jones, Sr. used to give an illustration about how a man and his wife have a fuss at home over coffee in the morning. The man snorts, and she pouts. He storms out the door and gets on the bus to go to work. There is a nice lady sitting on the bus. "Oh, good morning," she says. And he thinks, "How nicely she speaks to me." Oh, if he only had a wife who would speak nicely in the morning. Then the man and the other woman meet for lunch, and the friendship develops. But this is where the old-fashioned home built on the Word of God makes the difference. The man's godly training rises in him. He realizes his error, breaks off the friendship, and makes things right at home. When things don't go well with your husband, get them patched in a hurry with the Word of God, and resist the devil. Perhaps someone at the office acts particularly friendly or compliments you on your dress, and your husband hasn't given you a compliment for so long you can't remember the last time (no thanks for the dinner, no notice of the dress, no recognition for anything), and you think, "Wouldn't it be wonderful if my husband would notice a little." But you control your mind and thoughts and stay true. The mind can wander so easily, and that is how the devil gets in and makes havoc of a home. None is invincible except by the grace of God. "Taking the shield of faith, wherewith ye shall be able to quench all the fiery darts of the wicked" (Eph. 6:16). Be bathed in the Word and in prayer, so that you respond only to the Lord and His call and to your husband and the things which are godly and right, so that your husband can "safely trust" his wife.

"I do" is said, and the preacher, as the minister of the gospel and the officer of the law, says, "I now pronounce you man and wife," and "til death do you part." That's it! Your shopping days are over! You don't have the right of thirty-day trial. You don't have the right of taking him back for a refund. It's settled. Be sure you are doing right. Be sure you are doing God's will when you marry, and then be loyal to your husband one hundred percent no matter what comes. Your whole Christian testimony is at stake as well as your marriage. What unsaved couple will consider their need of the Saviour if they see the same flaws in your marriage as in their own? It would seem impossible for Christians to have such problems, yet I could tell you some heartbreaking instances where marriages have sunk in deep trouble. For example, I know of a young couple who got at odds with each other, and it just looked as if they couldn't make it. At last they went to the pastor for help as a marriage counselor. Well, it was some kind of counseling. That couple ended up getting a divorce, and she married the counselor! Little children were hurt and a Christian ministry was brought to reproach, all because people who professed to be Christians had learned neither loyalty nor self-control. What a tragedy!

In another situation the church secretary worked with the preacher in the church office. The secretary was always considerate and concerned for his needs. One thing led to another, and the pastor left his wife and married the secretary.

I know of one church where the same woman was responsible for three different preachers being ruined! You say, "She must have been some woman!" Yes, and I'm sure there were many facets to each of these incidents, but perhaps all of them could have been avoided if the men's wives had been warm, loving, considerate, and kind. Perhaps there would have been no stories to tell, no gossip for the neighbors to feast upon, no reproach brought to the Lord's name if those men's wives had put away self and put their husbands and their husbands' work and calling first. Perhaps a warm, selfless, loving, obedient wife at home could have made all the difference.

Submission

The next thing in which the wife will do her husband good and not evil all the days of her life is following the order of the home structure set down in Scripture. You see, a home has to be structured according to the Word of God. You cannot build a Christian home like Topsy and expect everything to come out all right. God gives us the order according to His Word, and part of it is found in Ephesians 5:21-23: "Submitting yourselves one to another in the fear of God. Wives, submit yourselves unto your own husbands, as unto the Lord. For the husband is the head of the wife, even as Christ is the head of the church: and he is the saviour of the body."

Those are beautiful verses, but I have seen women really rebel' at this scriptural injunction. Years ago in a revival meeting, my husband preached on the structure of the home, including women being in subjection to their husbands, "even as Sarah obeyed Abraham, calling him lord" (I Peter 3:6). There was almost a riot after the service out on the church steps, and the preacher's wife was leading it. With four or five other women, she was leading a rebellion. She had no intention of obeying the Word of God. And it was obvious in many ways. One night she stayed home from the meetings to clean house with the excuse of how many hours she had to work. She worked shift work. She did work hard, but that was no excuse. The rebellion showed in her and in the children. The pastor's children were lost to the world because they didn't want anything to do with religion. Is it any wonder when they saw such conflict in the home with such a rebellious mother? This couple's children were in chaos on the inside. It is a wonder more kids don't end up in the psychiatrist's office when you see that kind of conflict even in a so-called Christian home.

Now if you rebel at this passage of Scripture, don't ever marry. Don't ever get married unless you have found a man you can love and honor and obey and respect because, according to God's Word, ladies, this is our responsibility. We are to submit ourselves to our husbands and be obedient. You wouldn't argue about whether or not we ought to obey the Lord, would you? You say, "Oh, if it says so in the Bible, then we have to do it. But if my husband says it, he can go jump in the lake, thank you." Whoa! We are to submit and obey as if we were obeying God Himself. That's the injunction, and we can have no argument with it.

You may say, "Why did God put me under such a command?" Well, you have to have order or you will have chaos. God made woman for man, not man for woman. In Genesis 2:18, the Scripture says, "And the Lord God said, It is not good that the man should be alone; I will make him an help meet for him." That verse is often read as if "help meet" were one word, but that is not it. She is to be a help, "meet" or "suited" for him, cut out to meet his needs. God picks a wife that will be best suited to help a man in the ministry or in the work of life that God has called him to do.

Another reason we are put under the injunction to obey and submit is not a very pretty reason, but we have to face it. It is in Genesis 3:16: "Unto the woman he said, I will greatly multiply thy sorrow and thy conception; in sorrow thou shalt bring forth children; and thy desire shall be to thy husband, and he shall rule over thee." We are to be in subjection because of the woman's part in the first sin. If Eve had not partaken of the fruit, if she had not offered it to Adam, we do not know what the end of the story might have been. But she did it, and God judged her, and, as her daughters, we are all judged and being judged. Of all the people in the world who ought to be thankful for the gospel of the Lord Jesus Christ, of all people who ought to be thankful that Jesus loved them and died for them, it ought to be women. Yet women can often be the most hardhearted. Yet, as I think about it, I don't see how a woman could help but love the Lord and run to Him when she sees from what He has redeemed her. What girl or woman is not constantly reminded of her sinful condition and her need of the Saviour? We are reminded every month! The pain, the nervousness, the upset, and the discomfort that we face every month is a direct result of this: "I will greatly multiply thy sorrow and thy conception." God set into motion something that would remind women of their utter dependence on the Lord and of their sinful nature. Except for the grace and mercy of God, what would our condition be? However, we should train our daughters to handle this ordinary occurrence discreetly and go on as usual.

God reminds women of their sinfulness in the pain and travail of childbirth. Bringing a child into the world reminds a woman of her sinful state and the reason for the trouble way back in the book of Genesis: "In sorrow thou shalt bring forth children" (Genesis 3:16). We women can never get away from the fact that it was our own weakness and the weakness in Eve that fell prey to the devil and brought on all the troubles in the beginning. We, of all people, ought to be mindful of what the Lord Jesus Christ did for us on the cross of Calvary. We, of all people, ought to be intent on obeying the Word of God and walking with the Lord.

Also it is good for you often to think about your husband and what he means to you. Sometimes you get so busy you forget to appreciate that man God gave you. You are so busy paying bills, keeping the schedule around the clock, and tending to endless duties that sometimes your husband doesn't get the appreciation he deserves. Stop and think. Who else provides for you like your husband? Who else puts the money in the bank so you could buy material for that new spring dress? Who else puts the groceries in the refrigerator and pantry? Stop, and take stock of the good blessings the Lord has given you in that man. He is the father of your children, and he loves you, even when you are sick, even when you are too tired to move, even when you come in and your hair looks like Phyllis Diller's! He's the man you love, and he loves you. Now, make him important in your life. Be ready for him when he comes home. Freshen up and try to look nice when he walks in the door. Don't be irritable as if to say, "Good grief! Is it time for you to come home already?" Be there with a smile and a warm welcome, so that when he sees you he thinks, "Man, that's the best gal in the world. I surely am glad the Lord gave her to me!" Make him glad to be home so that it doesn't matter how many beautiful women there are in the world or how many have more money or talents, he would rather have you than anybody on the face of God's earth.

Now don't get what I'm saying about sprucing up and being sharp when your husband comes home mixed up with a sensual philosophy that is presented in a current best seller—a so-called Christian book for women. The philosophy that a Christian wife should be sensual is dangerous and wrong, yet it is being pawned off on Christian women in many churches. They are buying copies of the book by the thousands. They are spending God's money to buy the printed literature and even to bring the workshops into churches. It is just an excuse for Christians to read and dwell on sensual, worldly ideas and justify themselves by saying it was written by a Christian for Christians. Christians, non-Christians, singles, marrieds, women living with men outside marriage, women living with other women's husbands—all can attend the workshop sessions without any conviction of sin. They just get help with their sex life and supposedly learn how to please the men whether their relationship is moral or not. If some of the advice were not so serious and deadly, it would be funny. Can you imagine a grown woman meeting her husband, who has just come in out of five o'clock rush traffic or from the manufacturing plant with his lunch box still in his hand, in nothing but baby blue baby-doll pajamas and white boots?

I say spruce up for your husband. Look clean and soft and feminine, but don't be ridiculous. Listen, if Christian women followed that devilish teaching, they would bring the atmosphere of the basement bar and the darkened liquor lounge into their homes. Their minds would be so eaten with sensual, gutter-level, fleshly, worldly thoughts that there would be no room for scriptural, godly thinking. Don't fall for that line of trying to be a sensual wife to keep your husband happy and interested. It is degrading; it is unscriptural. The Christian wives' behavior is to "be sober, to love their husbands, to love their children, To be discreet, chaste, keepers at home, good, obedient to their own husbands, that the word of God be not blasphemed" (Titus 2:4-5). "Whose adorning let it not be that outward adorning of plaiting the hair, and of wearing of gold, or of putting on of apparel; But let it be the hidden man of the heart, in that which is not corruptible, even the ornament of a meek and quiet spirit, which is in the sight of God of great price" (I Peter 3:3-4).

If your husband is a Christian, then heaven is his home, and heaven is going to be wonderful. In the meantime, make your Christian home here as close to heaven as you possibly can. Make home a haven of rest. They say a man's home is his castle. That mostly depends upon his wife. You don't need a million-dollar estate or a one-hundred-thousand-dollar mansion. A four-room bungalow can be the best place on earth if a wife and husband are together and the Lord Jesus Christ is the center of their home.

Obedience

In the oft-diluted marriage vows pronounced at many modern weddings, the bride promises to "love, honor, and cherish," and the promise "to obey" is strikingly missing. Yet this scriptural premise cannot be ignored regardless of man's (or woman's) efforts to cancel it in today's marriages. Neither the "enlightenment" of modern education nor the pressures of NOW, the National Organization for Women, HEW, ERA, nor any other women's liberation effort can cancel God's divine injunction to wives to be "obedient to their own husbands" (Titus 2:5). Willing obedience to your husband is yet another way to do your husband good. This command does not allow disobedience because you are not in the mood, because his request doesn't harmonize with your schedule, because you feel the demand is foolish or unreasonable, because you feel it is a selfish demand, because you feel it is a waste of time or money, because you simply "don't want to." In God's order of the home, the woman is to obey the head, the man. Old-fashioned? It is as up-to-date as today's sunshine—and just as important and blessed to a Christian home. Trust your husband's judgment. Do it his way. Obey willingly.

If vacation time comes, go camping to the mountains with him, even if you would rather vacation in a nice air-conditioned beach house. You will not die of bug bites or inconveniences. You had better be glad he wants you to go along. You know, he could leave you at home to work and tend the children while he went camping with friends. You had better pack up your gear and be glad to go.

Perhaps he feels you need to see a doctor. You may think your physical problem is not that serious. You may dread or even fear to go to the doctor, but if your husband tells you to go, you must obey.

The living room suite may be threadbare, scratched, and dilapidated. You may want to buy a new one. Perhaps there is little money available, but you insist that you could pay a small down payment and handle the balance in monthly payments. Your husband, on the other hand, insists that the budget cannot afford the payments, and he resents the high interest rate on such an arrangement. Suppose he will not give his consent to the purchase until there is cash on hand. Then you have to be obedient and wait for the new furniture. In the meantime, make the old pieces look as good as you can; pray that the Lord will supply the money for the new set if it is His will; but most important—wait patiently and sweetly, not with a cold, griping attitude. Outward obedience with an inward uncooperative, negative attitude is still rebellion, and God is not likely to bless such a situation.

Perhaps your work looms high before you, and you feel you must stay up late night after night to finish. Perhaps your husband finally says that you must stop and go to bed and get some rest. Though the work is important, you must obey your husband and get the needed rest.

On the other hand, perhaps you have worked until you are bone-tired and feel you can go no further. Yet perhaps there is a deadline to meet and a great urgency in the task, and your husband asks or even insists that you stick to it, that you keep on working until the job is done. Then your rest and comfort will have to wait. You must cooperate and obey your husband with a willing heart.

In all situations, be a cooperative, considerate, obedient wife. Even many unsaved husbands have been won to the Lord by the gracious testimony of a loving, obedient wife. Don't let your personal wants interfere with your marriage relationship. Your will is to be subordinate and submissive to his.

Accountability

Now just a word of caution. There have been some well-meaning Christians who seem to have carried the matter of obedience to what I believe to be an extreme position. Obedience to your husband is mandatory, and we cannot take away any weight from that precept; however, some have felt that God means for wives to obey their husbands even when their command is morally wrong and contrary to the Word of God. Now marriage does not mean that the wife forgets scriptural convictions and instructions and is relieved of her individual responsibility to God. There are no conflicts in the Word of God. To obey your husband does not mean to reject other clear commands of Scripture.

Ephesians 5:22-24 does not cancel other passages of
Scripture such as Exodus 20:13-15: "Thou shalt not
kill. Thou shalt not commit adultery. Thou shalt not
steal." Though the possibility seems remote, if an
unsaved husband should for whatever reason
demand that his Christian wife do any of those acts
which are clearly in conflict with the holy commands
of God's Word, the Christian wife's responsibility is
to obey God. In God's order of the structure of the
home, man is over woman, and God is over man.
God never relinquishes His authority. He is the final
word in every matter, and if man's will and word
cross God's Word, then the woman must obey
God. Those who say that the wife must do the
husband's command, even if it is morally wrong and
contrary to the Bible, reason that God will somehow
intervene in the matter to keep her from having to
do wrong or that God will overrule and not hold her
responsible. Perhaps in some cases He will
intervene, but I can find no Scripture to guarantee
such intervention. This would seem to be rather
presumptive ground on which to stand. God said in
Deuteronomy 6:16, "Ye shall not tempt the Lord
your God." Jesus repeated it: "It is written again,
Thou shalt not tempt the Lord thy God" (Matt. 4:7).
We should not presume on God; we are to follow
His precepts: "Ye shall diligently keep the
commandments of the Lord your God, ... And
thou shalt do that which is right and good in the sight
of the Lord" (Deut. 6:17, 18).

Dr. Bob Jones, Sr. said it in two words—words
applicable to any situation—"Do right!" It is simple
and clear. As a Christian wife you are to obey

explicitly the wishes and commands of your husband no matter how large or small as long as they do not cause you to violate the commands of Scripture. If the time should come when you are faced with being told to do something that you know is contrary to God's Word, you should first do your best to try to help your husband see your position: the thing he asks is in violation to your understanding of God's Word. You should handle it as sweetly, as quietly, as humbly as humanly possible. You should discuss the problem only with your husband or pastor. You should not tell your children and cause a conflict between their father and them because of your problem. You should not tell the neighbor women or the girls where you work or the women at church, or in any way make public that which is a private matter. Try to help your husband see that you have been obedient and cooperative in every area that you can, that you would obey him in this point if it were possible, but that you cannot disobey God's Word. He may respect your convictions and honor your stand. If he should yet be unyielding in his demand, then you would have to stand firmly and disobey him and take whatever consequences may come.

Just suppose your husband says you should have an abortion. Your responsibility is to show him sensibly in a humble attitude how this is wrong according to the Scriptures. If at last he will not yield, you will have to take your stand. Abortion is murder.

If he has no spiritual perception and wants you as a Christian wife to put on a miniskirt and go dancing with him at a night club, what should be your

position? First, you must quietly, gently, humbly try
to show him that you do not want to do this,
because it is contrary to God's instruction to
Christian women. As a Christian you are to dress
modestly. You are to be found in the right places.
Your place is not dancing in a nightclub under any
circumstances. Plead with him; reason with him.
Yet if he will not change his mind, you have to take
your stand for the Lord Jesus Christ.

This is why obedience every day in every other
matter is so important. Go with him when he wants
you to go to the ballgame; go with him when he
wants you to go fishing or hiking or shopping or
cattle buying. Do everything he wants you to do that
is right and honorable willingly and happily, so that if
a situation arises in which you cannot obey because
of the boundaries of the Word of God, he will know
your refusal to submit is because of genuine
scriptural conviction and not just because of your
personal will or desire in the matter. This kind of
consistent testimony gives God the opportunity to
use the crisis to work in your husband's heart and
life.

The same principle is true with children's obeying unsaved parents when told to do something
contrary to the Word. Do you see how far that line
of thinking could lead? Listen, missionaries have
told of precious children who received the Lord
Jesus Christ as their Saviour, gave up their idols,
took their stand against heathenism and idolatry at
home, and took beatings unto blood and some even
unto death for their testimony's sake. Now if you
follow the soft line of thinking that says you just obey
whether or not a command is contrary to God's

Word, you are taking the backbone out of being a Christian. With that philosophy you could do anything anyone in authority over you told you to do with the excuse, "Well, he told me to." You would not have to stand for the Lord. You would not have to have any personal responsibility under God. If that philosophy were true, Shadrach, Meshach, and Abednego were foolish to be thrown into the fiery furnace. They could have just bowed because the king ordered them to do so. God would just have had to overlook their bowing to a false god because they obeyed the heathen authority over them. Now that is not biblical. It takes the backbone out of being a Christian. It takes away individual responsibility to God. It takes away the reproach of Christ. When your testimony for the Lord Jesus Christ is at stake, when it is a matter of right or wrong, you have to obey and stand clear-cut for God regardless of the cost.

Stewardship

"She seeketh wool, and flax, and worketh willingly with her hands. She is like the merchants' ships; she bringeth her food from afar. She riseth also while it is yet night, and giveth meat to her household, and a portion to her maidens. She considereth a field, and buyeth it: with the fruit of her hands she planteth a vineyard" (vv. 13-16). We are stewards. The Bible speaks of being stewards with money, but we are stewards also of our time and energy. The husband can go off to work in the morning, knowing that you will handle your time wisely. Consider how much time some women who do not work away from home spend before the television set every day. They get involved in the soap operas and live the experiences of the characters vicariously. It is detrimental to their family life and to their own spiritual condition. Television can rob us of time that we should spend not only in God's Word but on other important things.

Some women say, "Oh, I don't watch television. I read. I just spend my time reading." Yes, but you had better be sure you are reading the right kind of books. Wrong books can also be detrimental. Even some so-called Christian books are treacherous. You must be very careful what authors and publishers you read. Be careful where the book came from and what its philosophy is.

"She worketh willingly with her hands" (v. 13). Rebekah was a good example of this verse. She knew how to get up in the morning and get the work done and not wait around for someone to suggest every job or duty. When I was a child, my piano teacher drilled, "Be your own worst critic. If you will criticize yourself and find your faults, the judge won't have to criticize you so harshly." That is good advice throughout life. Be your own worst critic about your house. If you will judge the cobwebs, the dust, and the ironing, if you will judge yourself and get the work done, then the Lord will not have to judge you. Your testimony will not be hampered as a result. Be a self-driver. "She worketh willingly with her hands." Our children need to be taught this principle also. Don't wait for someone to assign you a job. Be the kind of person who sees a job and does it for herself. Get on the job, move out, and do it without having to be prodded.

Nutrition

"She is like the merchants' ships; she bringeth her food from afar" (v. 14). In the day this was written, people had to scout for food. Now you have your garden and the grocery store, but still the concerned wife takes time to think and plan for economy and nutrition in the menus for the week and groceries for the month. Cooking is more than filling hollow legs. Cooking is good food served with love and joy. Your time at the table and in the kitchen with your family is very important. There are things that are taught there that cannot be communicated as well any other time. Make much of the time with your girls when you are cooking. Make much of suppertime with your family. Take time and care to teach good manners. Make mealtime a time your boys and girls will remember, and let your cooking be stirred with love.

Be sure your meals are planned with concern for your family's health. Plan, too, for your children's afternoon snacks. It is so easy to depend on quick, commercial snack foods, but far better it is for Mother to have fresh fruit or vegetables ready with milk or fruit juice when those "famished troops" burst in from school. Children can easily fill up on chips and soft drinks and by mealtime not really be interested in foods needed for healthy bodies. We need to be concerned about the right kind of cooking in a Christian home.

"She riseth also while it is yet night, and giveth meat to her household, and a portion to her maidens" (v. 15). I wrote earlier of the importance of getting up early and having devotions while the house is still quiet, before the children are running around looking for their socks or misplaced homework papers. Before all that commotion begins, get by yourself in a corner somewhere and study the Word of God and spend time in prayer. Without it, you are not prepared. No matter how fancy a breakfast you fix for your children or how smoothly their clothes are ironed, if you are not prepared spiritually to meet them and send them off to school with a covering of prayer, you are not prepared, and they aren't either. How can we expect to meet the demands and problems of the day without time with the Lord? It is simply impossible.

"And giveth meat to her household" (v. 15). Breakfast is essential. I understand some children cannot eat as much as others, and I wouldn't want them to eat thirty-eight pancakes every morning like Sambo. But I think there is a sense in which you must watch a child's diet. If children overeat and get too chubby when they are little, eating too much will be a problem for them when they are grown. Watching diet is important. Some parents spoil their children in the name of love by giving them all the little goodies they want and developing a weakness which will later give them a problem in controlling their weight. This is an area we must watch because children need a good, wholesome, hearty breakfast to stabilize them and get them set for the day's work. So rise up early.

Economy

"She considereth a field, and buyeth it; with the fruit of her hands she planteth a vineyard" (v. 16). Her husband can trust her judgment; she will not squander money. In fact, she will be careful how she spends it, so that she will have a little profit. With this profit she can "consider a field and buy it" or "plant a vineyard," or in some useful way bring in more profit for the family. Her husband can trust her economically. She will not race to see how much she can spend every month but will handle the money wisely. She will look for ways to make the income even more profitable than it initially seems to be.

Physical Fitness

"She girdeth her loins with strength, and strengtheneth her arms" (v. 17). She is as physically fit as possible. She does not let herself become lazy and fat and flabby. She is careful to get the exercise she needs, to eat right, and to be as physically healthy as possible. Married or not, that is the responsibility of a Christian woman. "What? know ye not that your body is the temple of the Holy Ghost which is in you, which ye have of God, and ye are not your own? For ye are bought with a price: therefore glorify God in your body, and in your spirit, which are God's" (I Cor. 6:19-20).

Self-discipline is necessary with our bodies. Your body is to be used for the Lord. It is to be as strong as possible to do the work of God as well as possible. Do whatever you know to do to keep yourself healthy and strong. When you are tired physically, that is the easiest time for the devil to attack. When you are sick, when you are running low, when you feel all washed out, that is when the devil will make everything seem out of proportion. You will be easily offended. You will be irritable. So it is important to be as strong as possible physically.

Good physical conditioning is important also to the control of the mind. Outward actions and emotions are first conceived in the mind, which must be kept under control. You cannot entertain questionable thoughts. You must put your mind on Scripture and spiritual things or get busy planning the next menu or consider what color to paint the bathroom. Control your mind so that it can be controlled by the Holy Spirit.

Encouragement

"She girdeth her loins with strength" (v. 17). She has a good attitude. She knows the truth of Romans 8:28: "And we know that all things work together for good to them that love God, to them who are the called according to his purpose." Now whether the car breaks down in the middle of the intersection or the sink won't drain or the bathroom is clogged or the rabbits ate every row of beans in the garden she knows that Romans 8:28 still stands. "Well," you say, "it's easy to quote that verse until something happens to me, and then it is another story." But we have to know it, not only in word, but also in our hearts, so that we can have the right attitude and trust the Lord. Instead of meeting Monday morning with a long face and a defeated spirit, "gird up your loins with strength." Call on the grace of God; head out the door; and don't let the devil whip you.

Be an encourager to your husband. When he comes home discouraged by low production or by a disagreement with the boss or by a refusal for a pay raise, encourage him. There is your chance to be encouraging rather than barking back with, "Well, if you think you had a bad day, listen to what happened here!" When things seem to go wrong and tough times come, stand steady, and by God's grace, be a leveling force and an encourager. Sometimes you don't even need to say a word; your smile will say, "Well, I know it will be all right. The Lord will work it out some way." Perhaps the situation is so big that you could not begin to untangle it, but you can pray. You can trust God, and He can lift the load. He can make your husband's burden light.

Be an encourager to your children. Take the edge off teasing. Don't let every incident be earthshaking. If the milk spills, don't have a spasm. Call the cat! Don't let your children be moody or feel sorry for themselves or think they got a raw deal from a friend, teacher, preacher, or employer. No matter what difficult situations we got into as children, my mother was never sympathetic. (If she was, we never knew it.) She always chided, "Never mind. It's good experience." We grew up on "good experience!" Sometimes I thought "good experience" would kill me. But Mother was right. I survived, and all those problems and obstacles were indeed good experience. We learned to square our shoulders and, by the grace of God, meet ever-changing demands.

Compassion

"She stretcheth out her hand to the poor; yea, she reacheth forth her hands to the needy" (v. 20). How expressive of the heart are the hands. My mother's hands are precious. She is now eighty-five years young and of very fair complexion. Her hands are a testimony of a life of self-sacrifice and service. They represent years of hard work from before dawn to past dark on the farm cooking for farm hands, gardening, canning and preserving food to provide the needs of family and friends, sewing, quilting, and making comforters. At a time in church work when little or nothing was being done for young people, least of all for country young people, she was ever arranging gospel programs and providing parties and outings to stir their interest. Her hands speak of countless hours spent caring for missionaries and for the sick and dying, getting supplies and tending business for those who could not help themselves, taking to heart and caring for the unfortunate family down the road whose strange background and training made them oddities and misfits in the community. Her time seemed to belong to those who needed her. Her compassionate hands tenderly washed and doctored the sores and diseased flesh that seemed untouchable to others.

There's no touch like Mother's touch when you are sick and her hand rests on your fevered brow. There is no touch like Mother's touch when she puts butter on the bump on your head after your fall down seventeen stairsteps. If a giant goose egg swelled on our forehead after such a fall, the first thing Mother did was to get a little butter out of the icebox and smooth it into the bump. I'm sure it was Mother's touch and attention that healed the hurt far more than the butter. Those hands, those precious hands!

Hands speak of giving, and that's really what the Christian life is all about. Your life is a constant giving out. Oh, yes, the children put a lot of love back in. They love you, and many times they are a pure joy to your heart, but most of the process is giving out, self-sacrifice. And that's what a woman's life ought to be. She stretches out her hands to the poor. This is the difference between a Christian woman, who is dedicated to the Lord, and non-Christian modern women who chatter about our liberties, our rights, our pay, and our demands. Such women are looking out for themselves, an attitude which is as opposite from the Christian viewpoint and Bible philosophy as anything could be. If you stand for the Lord and by the Book, you are going to be a misfit in this world. You might as well get used to it and say, "Lord, here I stand. Let people think what they will."

Be there with a helping hand when neighbors are sick or bereaved. Don't wait for someone else to take the responsibility. You can be a testimony and an encouragement. There may be unsaved family members who are watching. They will recognize and remember the Christian friend who was there in the time of need. In a time of sickness or death, in a time of physical need or problems, your quiet presence, a few groceries from your pantry, or something warm from your oven could mean more than words could express. "Withhold not good from them to whom it is due, when it is in the power of thine hand to do it." This is part of your testimony for the Lord.

Prayer support is also a way you can stretch out your hands to the poor and needy. Some people have no one to pray for them but you. There may be unsaved loved ones or neighbors who have no one else who cares for their souls, and prayer is a powerful way in which you can reach out your helping hand. Another means of offering help is through your compassionate heart. Your heart can offer understanding and your ear can be open to the needy's cry. Be an encourager and make every effort to lift others. Always remember, except for the grace of God, you could be in as great need or worse. Have a compassionate heart.

We need compassion to stretch out our hands to the unsaved. This is a need greater than physical food and care or financial security. The best help you can be to any unsaved person is to tell him about the Saviour. Keep some tracts in your purse. Be ready to witness. Have a compassionate, warm, alert heart to one in need of the Lord Jesus Christ. The Lord must prepare the situation, but if you are yielded to the Holy Spirit, you can be the one to bring the message when that heart is ready. Be prepared to give the salvation message at any time. Keep a little Wordless Book in your purse. You never know when you are going to meet a child. He may be bouncing like a Mexican jumping bean, but a Wordless Book or other object may attract his attention and make him stand still and listen. You may get the opportunity to give him the gospel and win him to the Lord right there. Dr. Henry Grube, preacher, Bible teacher, and early advocate of Christian education for elementary-age children, in his busy schedule always seemed to take time with little children. He always carried a little trick of some kind in his pocket. In an unsuspecting instant, he would capture children's attention and give them the gospel. Be watching for opportunities. You may be working out in your garden picking beans and resenting the bugs, when suddenly some children will come by on bicycles. There's your opportunity.

Let the Lord make opportunities for you. You may be surprised at the situations and opportunities He will set up for you if you are sincere in praying for opportunities and take them when they come. Be a soulwinner. The women of the world are busy building their houses, decorating and redecorating, and gaining possessions for this life, but we need to have matters of eternal value on our hearts and minds.

Lasting Treasure

Some would gather money
  along the path of life;
Some would gather roses
  and rest from worldly strife.

But I would gather children
  From among the thorns of sin;
I would seek a golden curl
  And a freckled, toothless grin.

For money cannot enter
  In that land of endless day;
Roses that are gathered
  Soon will wilt along the way.

But, oh, the laughing children,
  As I cross the sunset sea:
Gates swing wide to Heaven,
  I can take them in with me!

—Billy Davis

Watch for some children that you can take to heaven with you, but watch for some grownups, too, who have hungry hearts. They may be laughing or carrying on business and showing little interest in spiritual matters, but beneath the surface you may find a hungry heart. Ask God to make you the epitome of Proverbs 31:20, stretching forth your hands to the needy, especially those who need the Saviour.

Appropriate Dress

"She is not afraid of the snow for her household: for all her household are clothed with scarlet. She maketh herself coverings of tapestry; her clothing is silk and purple" (vv. 21-22). These verses and verse 25 speak of a woman's apparel.

First, you will notice she is not afraid for her household. Her first thought is not for herself but for her children and her family. As Christian mothers in this day, we have a responsibility to teach our children to dress modestly and in line with the Word of God. The pressure from the world is to look like the world, to wear as little as you can get by with, and to look as tacky as possible. The pressure from the stores and manufacturers is terrific. Some time ago we looked for a ready-made skirt for a teenage girl. The search was futile. The girls' departments were full of "jeans britches" sewed inside-out with ragged, frayed edges all around. They looked like candidates for rags for a car wash but were priced at fifteen dollars. The world established that trash as the style for teenagers. Now as Christian parents we have an obligation to set higher standards for our young people according to the Word of God and not allow them to follow worldly fads.

Little girls need to know that they wear dresses except when certain work or activities call for culottes or other suitable attire because of modesty. You have to train children. If they are allowed to dress sloppily and immodestly all of the time, they will dread having to put on something decent and dress neatly for Sunday school. I don't think they should wear their Sunday best seven days a week, but they ought to dress cleanly, neatly, and modestly. Such training will affect them all their lives.

We also have to teach them what is appropriate for the occasion. Playclothes are okay for the beach but not for school or town. One morning I saw a girl on her way to school. I suppose I should have been glad that she was modestly clad, but her outfit was difficult to believe. Paint the mental picture if you will of a nice, decent dress with a baseball cap, loud, sporty, striped knee socks, and two-inch heels! If she had been dressing to play a comic in a junior-high skit, she couldn't have done a better job. The sad part was that she didn't have a mother who loved her enough to say, "Now, dear, high heels are appropriate for church or dress-up, but when you go to school you need to dress appropriately." The girl needed to know that knee socks go with certain sport clothes and stockings are for dress clothes. You would think that proper dress would be second-nature, but, if you don't teach your children both by example and by instruction, they will lack in good taste and know-how concerning their clothes. Young girls also need to learn to sit in a modest and lady-like position at all times. Carelessness in sitting is a comfort no lady can afford. Clothing affects attitude, manners, posture, and quality of work, and is an integral part of child training.

The passage does not say she was concerned about the clothing of her children only. Verse 21 says her "household," so that includes her husband.

Some wives are so busy getting dolled up themselves that their husband's wardrobe has to get together the best it can. Some men are very conscious of what they wear, but some are not. Then it falls upon your shoulders to help keep his clothes like they ought to be. Look for the frayed collar. Get him a new shirt if he needs one. Encourage him to buy the new suit if the other one is old and it's just time to get a new one, even if he insists the old one is still hanging together and is good enough. Help your husband look as well dressed as possible because that's part of his testimony, too. If he doesn't seem to have time to see that his shoes are shined, then you see about it. Be sure his socks are matched. Don't wait for him to rumble through the drawer in the morning half asleep, hoping his socks are matched and right side out. Be sure they are right when you put them away. Touch up the wash-'n-wear collar with the iron. It is a wife's responsibility to see that her man looks good. Don't say, "Well, he's a grown man; he can tend to it himself." Remember, you are his help meet, his help, meet for him, matched to his needs. A later verse in Proverbs 31 says, "Her husband is known in the gates." How he looks does matter.

"She maketh herself coverings of tapestry; her clothing is silk and purple" (v. 22). Her clothing is not necessarily expensive, but it is neat, sharp, colorful, and appropriate for the occasion. How you dress is one of the easiest ways to state your testimony, especially in this day when standards are so low. Women wear slacks, shorts, and some of the worst outfits possible. You wonder how they have nerve to wear such combinations at home, let alone in public. It's like that little quip in the newspaper: "If some women had better hindsight, they wouldn't wear so many tight slacks!" You get the view they don't! They are stating what they are and what they want to be. If you want by first meeting and first impression to have a testimony that says, "I'm a Christian woman who knows how to behave," then dress accordingly. There was a bit of a stir about a judge in Ohio who dismissed charges in the rape case of a fifteen-year-old boy against a girl after seeing her first in public. When the matter came to the judge, he just turned the boy loose. In essence he said that in this permissive society, the boy did what came naturally and women ask for it by their dress and manner of living. Perhaps it is unfortunate that a judge would not protect people more than that, but I see his point. By their tight, immodest apparel, low-cut or see-through blouses, many women purposely invite the attention of men; then when the response gets out of hand, they scream for protection. The women's liberationists want women to be "free," but when they get in trouble they want the judge to protect them. How foolish! If a woman wants to dress and look like an animal, don't be surprised when she gets treated like one. In this permissive, loose society where the standards of the Word of God have been put away, don't be surprised when women reap the consequences.

So it is very important that women dress modestly. You are a testimony first of all for the Lord, but you are also a testimony for your husband. People are getting an impression of your husband by how you dress, how you walk, how you talk, and how you behave. At a funeral last summer, one woman stood out like a sore thumb. She wore a dress with a short, short skirt, and the low neckline almost met the hemline. Her attire looked as if it belonged in the dark corners of a night club rather than in the bright daylight, let alone at such a solemn occasion. The purpose was obvious. It was obvious, too, that some of the men present followed their instincts. Little by little, she got the attention she sought. That is unfortunate. I couldn't help but feel sorry for her even though her attire was terribly inappropriate. How we dress speaks before a word is spoken. It affects our testimony and is ever important.

Exalting Your Husband

"Her husband is known in the gates" (v. 23). Listen, that's what this whole chapter in Proverbs is about. It has been speaking of the wife, what she is and what she does, but the purpose and goal of it all is for her husband, for her home, and for the Lord. As evidenced by this verse, all she does is not to point up herself, but her whole calling is to enhance her husband: spotlight his talents, highlight his strengths, and be interested in his sitting in the gate.

What are some practical ways a Christian wife can exalt her husband? What are some ways she can put him "in the gate"? Here are some suggestions at least for a beginning.

1. *Honor him by your signature.* Sign your name as his wife. When you are writing personal friends or jotting off a quick note, you may want to sign your own first name, but in a business or formal capacity it is an honor to your husband when you sign "Mrs. Robert Williams" rather than "Susie

Williams." Sign in his name, and the reader's first thought is of your husband and secondly of you. You immediately bring honor to him through your signature.

2. *Lift him up to the children.* Never undercut their father to them. Never question before them his decision or why or how he did something. Do not in any way put a thought in the children's minds that you are not behind him all the way or that you disagree with something he said. Now, if you disagree, talk with him about it privately and get the question settled, but don't ever let the children see division between you and him. I think of a situation when a boy did not do well on a test at school. He had told his father the night before that he needed to study, but the father insisted the boy work with him. The mother afterwards told the son, "Now the next time something like that happens, I mean for you to tell me." Do you see that she immediately exalted herself to the child above her husband? Don't undercut your husband to the children.

3. *Give him attention at home.* Children need attention, but they also have to give attention to their father. The Word says, "Honor thy father and thy mother." Much of honoring the father will be taught by you. When he comes into the house, Dad's chair should be vacant and waiting. That's his chair. There are certain things that the family sets apart because "they're Dad's." He is given the proper attention, respect, and immediate, unquestioned obedience.

4. *Make home pleasant.* Don't bombard your husband with every unthinkable trouble you had all day the minute he steps in the door. Make home a

haven.

5. *Support his interests.* Men have to have an outlet for their energy and a change of pace from routine. You might like your husband to come home and help with the myriad of details there, but when he has been at work all day sometimes he just needs to do something else—garden, golf, fish, or build. Don't downgrade his hobby or interest, or it will become a division between you. Support him in his outside interests.

6. *Don't let others make even teasing remarks concerning him in your presence.* Now when he is right in the middle of the conversation and the men are joking back and forth at each other, that's one thing. But don't let them tease about him to you if he is not there. Even in a joking manner, never let him be referred to as "your old man." Straighten out the ill-mannered speaker quickly. Don't ever let anyone think that your husband is an "old man" or that he or she can make light of him in your presence.

7. *Never speak when it is his place to speak.* I could tell of more than one young couple in which the woman puts her husband in a bad light because she speaks too soon. The woman is more outgoing than the man. If they are standing together and someone asks a question, she immediately expounds the answer. Swallow it, squash it, choke on it, but keep still! Your husband may be slow to speak, but when he speaks it will probably be worth hearing. Give him time to say it. You don't have to answer every question or speak on every subject. There will be time for you to add your comments if necessary.

8. *Don't interrupt when he is speaking.* This is important as an example before your children as well as a courtesy to him. For instance, if your husband is in conference or just visiting with other men, stand quietly and wait until he sees and recognizes you before you speak. Unless the building is on fire or a child has been injured or some extreme emergency has occurred, be recognized before you speak. Never burst in with "Hey, let me tell you something" or "Sign this quickly, will you?" Don't interrupt a man when he is talking with other men. Show him respect.

9. *Never boss him.* A back-seat driver in private may cause untold damage, but a boss in public is fatal. Men are embarrassed by wives who give bossy commands in public or in front of other men. Don't forget, you have a reputation with your husband's friends and associates. You say, "Well, that's ridiculous. It's none of their business." Maybe not, but they make it their business. Much of their respect for a man is based on his wife's manner. They know if he has a bossy wife who expects him to step lively when she speaks. It brings embarrassment to him. Never boss. Be careful how you state things to your husband, even if you are making a reasonable request.

10. *Be gracious and grateful.* Never *expect* help or assistance from your husband or from any other man. Be grateful and gracious when a man moves to help you. I know an attractive young lady who may never win a man's admiration let alone a husband's love unless her attitude changes toward a man's assistance. One day as she was carrying a large, heavy, awkward load, someone suggested to a

young man nearby, "Why don't you help her, Jack?" The girl's response was, "Yeah, Jack, why don't you help?" No wonder Jack had to be pressed to help her, especially if he had observed her attitude in similar situations previously. Well, Jack helped her all right, but whatever gentlemanly, chivalrous instincts he may have felt were no doubt killed by her ungrateful attitude. Never take a man or his assistance for granted.

11. *Pray for your husband.* Blessed is the man whose wife walks with him and with the Lord. Blessed is the man whose wife carries him on her heart in prayer. If no one supported your husband in prayer except you, how much would his name be held before the throne of grace? How many of his burdens could be lightened, how many difficulties overcome, how many problems solved, how many hurts healed by a merciful heavenly Father in answer to the prayers of a faithful wife? The kitchen may attract the most attention, and the family room may be the place to congregate, but the prayer closet is the most important room in your home.

12. *Think and consider.* With prayerful consideration, add your own suggestions to these to promote your husband that he may also "sit in the gate." The support of a faithful, obedient, gracious, loving wife makes a man a king wherever he is. "A virtuous woman is a crown to her husband" (Prov. 12:4), a crown whose value and beauty far exceed the worth of a sovereign's regal adornment.

Conclusion

Whirlwind courtship? Perhaps it seemed so to human eyes, but the marriage of Isaac and Rebekah was ordained of God in heaven. Two hearts proved their humility and obedience to the Lord, and in God's time, He brought them together, sealed their vows, and the "twain" became "one flesh." The Scripture brings to a climax the touching romance, gently draws the tent curtains on their wedding night, and in quiet eloquence utters the summary of it all. In exquisite simplicity and beautiful intimacy, which heaven alone could know, God breathed, "And he loved her."

Their life together held many joys and sorrows, many crests of victory and valleys of struggle, but their love for the God Who called them and their love for each other stemmed the changing tides of life's sea. "For love is strong as death; ... Many waters cannot quench love, neither can the floods drown it" (Song of Solomon 8:6, 7).

Through the eyes of Scripture, we view the scene as at her death Abraham mourns and weeps for Sarah and buries her in the cave of Machpelah; we share his sorrow as Jacob lays Rachel to rest on the way to Ephrath and marks her lonely grave with a pillar; but God shields from our eyes the earthly farewell of Isaac and Rebekah and graciously grants them silence and solitude in parting. It is not recorded in Holy Writ, but the heart somehow seems to sense one tender, unwritten epitaph, "And he loved her."

"And he loved her." What more could any wife desire? Whether a new bride or one of many years, as long as there is breath, it is never too late to make the most of every moment with your beloved. With genuine love to God and to your husband, fulfill to the utmost of your ability the commands and guidelines of God's Word as a Christian wife, so that you may have God's rich blessing now on your life and service together. Live so dedicated to the Lord Jesus Christ that your works and the fruit of your hands will bring praise and honor and glory unto Him. Live so humbly, so unselfishly, so devotedly to your husband, be such a "help meet for him" that whether silent or uttered, this crowning glory may also be yours—"And he loved her!"